Message from the Organization

We, the organization, wish to recognize the important role of those "advertisers" in today's society who provide the ongoing boost by constantly supporting projects like this.

We sincerely appreciate and thank all the merchants, business people, and others, whose fine spirit of co-operation made it possible for us to publish and market this book.

We truly hope that you will enjoy its use. Should you require extra copies of this publication for your friends, relatives or neighbors, you may purchase them from us.

The Organization
Whose Name Appears
On the Following Pages

This book was published for the organization by **GATEWAY PUBLISHING CO. LTD.**
811 Pandora Ave., W., Winnipeg, Manitoba R2C 2Z9

LITHO IN CANADA

Take time for 10 things

1 *Take time to Work —*
   it is the price of success.

2 *Take time to Think —*
   it is the source of power.

3 *Take time to Play —*
   it is the secret of youth.

4 *Take time to Read —*
   it is the foundation of knowledge.

5 *Take time to Worship —*
   it is the highway of reverence and washes
   the dust of earth from our eyes.

6 *Take time to Help and Enjoy Friends —*
   it is the source of happiness.

7 *Take time to Love —*
   it is the one sacrament of life.

8 *Take time to Dream —*
   it hitches the soul to the stars.

9 *Take time to Laugh —*
   it is the singing that helps with life's loads.

10 *Take time to Plan —*
   it is the secret of being able to have time
   to take time for the first nine things.

The Crete Municipal Hospital Auxiliary was organized in May, 1980. Its purpose is to "render service to Crete Municipal Hospital and its patients, and to assist the hospital in promoting the health and welfare of the community, in accordance with objectives established by the hospital."

The organization is open to active, as well as silent members, and currently boasts more than eighty on its roster.

Among annual projects undertaken by the auxiliary are: a bake and craft sale in December, support of the Health Fair, Hospital Employee Tea, Volunteer Yearly Awards Tea and the newest and most profitable - the Spring Tour of Homes.

Proceeds from the fund raisers have furnished the hospital with various pieces of equipment including: a rocker for new mothers; several infant car seats for rent to new families; sound projector and cassette player, to mention only a few. Perhaps the most impressive machine donated by auxiliary funds is the electronic blood pressure and pulse monitor.

Besides fund raising activities, the auxiliary publishes a bi-yearly NEWSLETTER; provides cookies for hospital sponsored activities, such as Open House, Retirement Teas, Supersitters Clinic, etc.; decorates the hospital at Christmas; and operates the gift cart service to the hospital.

Of course, not to be overlooked, are those ladies who so generously give of their time to staff the Information Desk, pass juice to patients and visitors, and provide coffee for families and friends.

The Crete Municipal Hospital Auxiliary is a caring, active organization. We appreciate your continued support by the purchase of this book.

Your **Gateway** *to* **Microwaving**

by
Sheryn Smith

Gateway Publishing Co. Ltd.
Winnipeg, Manitoba

ISBN: 0-920030-21-1

Printed and bound in Canada

This book is the culmination of many years work as a demonstrator for one of the largest microwave manufacturers in Japan, and many years of teaching microwave cooking to both adults and children. All the recipes have been tested, using 650 and 700 watt microwave ovens. Some are contributions from students, some are from other microwave demonstrators and teachers and many are those of my own creation, developed when microwave ovens were quite new and there were not too many microwave recipe books around. I hope you will enjoy using the book and perhaps develop a friendlier relationship with your microwave with the aid of the tips, hints, and information found between the covers.

Please keep in mind, that, as with any recipe book, you may wish to delete or add certain touches of your own. This is great, for this is how new recipes are developed. Further, due to the individual output and wattages of various manufacturers' microwave ovens, cooking times may vary. The ones suggested are only a guideline. Always cook to the minimum time called for in a recipe and add time thereafter. It is a good idea to mark any changes right beside the recipe for future reference.

Whether you live to eat or eat to live I hope that "Your Gateway to Microwaving" will whet your appetite and tickle your cooking fancy. Enjoy!

Sheryn Smith, Author

EGGS (continued)

FISH

BEEF

BEEF *(continued)*

PORK

POULTRY

POULTRY (continued)

CAKES (SWEETS)

CAKES *(continued)*

CANDY

COOKIES AND BARS

COOKIES AND BARS *(continued)*

DESSERTS

FRUITS

PIES

PIES (continued)

PUDDINGS AND CUSTARDS

QUICKBREADS AND MUFFINS

VEGETABLES

VEGETABLES *(continued)*

VEGETABLES *(continued)*

HOW DO MICROWAVES WORK?

Microwave ovens are made up of a cavity, where the food is cooked, a control panel, which commands the oven's operation, and a magnetron which produces the microwaves. The magnetron can be likened to the picture in a television set in that it is what makes the oven work. The magnetron emits high frequency radio waves, microwaves, which cause the molecules within the food to rotate 180 degrees two and a half billion times per second, creating friction, which causes heat. It is the same effect you get when you rub your hands together, the faster you rub them, the more friction there is and the hotter they get. The microwaves have much the same effect. The waves are about the thickness of a pencil and about three to four inches long and penetrate the food to about three quarters of an inch to one inch and the rest of the cooking process is done by conduction.

Conduction is the transfer of heat from one layer to the next, so, because the microwaves only penetrate the surface of the food, it is obvious that microwaves cook from the outside of the food surface into the core. Microwaves pass through substances such as wood, paper, glass and plastic, bounce off of metal and are absorbed by mass, such as meats, vegetables and liquids.

ARE MICROWAVES HARMFUL?

Of the many waves and rays which float through our atmosphere, there are two types of rays in particular with which we should be concerned. Firstly, there are ionizing rays in the atmosphere that are generated by x-rays, gamma rays, cosmic rays and ultraviolet rays. The ionizing rays store in the body and can damage chromosomes and cells. They accumulate in the body and that is why you will see lab technicians and other individuals who are constantly exposed to x-rays wearing little "badges" which monitor their exposure to these rays, to let them know when they have to be cautious against receiving any further ionizing rays. The second type of ray in this group is the non-ionizing ray, which does not store in the body and does not cause changes in the cells. Non-ionizing rays come from microwaves, radar, televisions and microwave towers. So, in that way, microwaves are not harmful to the body.

CAN A MICROWAVE OVEN REPLACE A CONVENTIONAL RANGE?

Although microwaves are a terrific tool in the kitchen, they are not the answer to every cooking situation. Puff pastries do not cook successfully in the microwave, nor does it work well for cooking eggs in the shell, angel or sponge cake, or for the deep frying of foods. Also, crusty foods require the dry heat of a conventional stove. So I think, as with every kitchen tool, microwave ovens have their place. Keep in mind, however, by using the microwave in conjunction with your conventional range you can often receive a very satisfactory result and save valuable time and energy.

DO I NEED TO GET NEW DISHES FOR MY MICROWAVE OVEN?

Probably not. There is a simple dish test that you can do to test the dishes you now have on hand which will allow you to see if they are microwave proof. Simply fill the dish half full with water and set in the oven. Microwave at full power for 2 minutes. The water should be getting slightly warm and the dish should remain cool where there is no water touching it. If the dish itself is very warm, then likely it has some metal content in its composition and should not be used in the oven. Glass, ceramic and porcelain are all good microwave ware provided they do not have a silver or gold trim . . . Ironstone and pottery are also good for microwave use for thawing and reheating, but ironstone usually has some metal content and over a long cooking period will become quite hot, so it is not recommended for cooking. Straw and wood are only appropriate for short reheating periods as the microwave tends to draw the moisture from the straw or wood, causing it to crack prematurely. On a wooden spoon or spatula handle this is not crucial, but on a steak board, one might consider another dish in its place. Plastics, other than those specifically designed for microwave use, again are only recommended for heating food products as the high temperature of the food may cause distortion of the container. When purchasing ovenware specifically for your microwave, try to purchase the type of material that is compatible for both microwave and conventional oven use. It is more economical in both terms of storage space and dollars.

PAPER, PLASTIC AND POTTERY - ARE THEY SAFE?

The question of using paper towels in the microwave is under constant debate. It seems that there have been reports of fires in microwave ovens during cooking with paper towels. After investigation, it was concluded that a metal impurity in the paper probably sparked the fire.

The general consensus is, however, that if pure, white, non-recycled paper is used, this lessens the chance of impurities in the paper. Paper with printed designs may have lead in the ink, so pure white paper is best.

This situation would apply to recipes telling you to cook in "a brown paper bag" - definitely a no-no!

Provided the paper towel will be in the oven less than four minutes it is likely safe to use. Waxed paper is an alternative to paper toweling.

When drying foods in the microwave it is best not to leave the oven in any case.

Plastics are a second issue. Baby bottles, for example, can be made of one of three plastic compounds. The first is polyethylene, the most common type of plastic liner. They come flat on a roll, perforated at intervals and sealed. This material is harmless, no matter how it is heated.

The second is polyvinyl chloride (PVC). This material is extremely hazardous, because infant formula contains liquids which extract PVC from the liner. You will notice a plastic odour when heated, and this type of plastic should never be used in the microwave.

The third type of plastic is rigid plastic, poly carb autoclavable, which is used to make the rigid, clear, reusable plastic bottles. These bottles can be microwaved, but they should be thrown out when they lose their clarity and become cloudy or show tiny fracture lines.

When heating formula in a bottle, be sure to shake it and test it on your wrist after 20 seconds, and then shake and test every 5 seconds thereafter. Never give the bottle to the baby before testing it.

Plastic containers in which margarine, dairy products and take out foods are packed are not recommended for microwave cooking, but they are useful. I cook, cool and store food in these containers for freezing. To microwave I simply pop the frozen lump into a microproof container and cook.

Paper take out packages contain glue, ink and dyes which can be absorbed into the foods, so it is best to transfer the foods into microproof dishes.

When purchasing paper plates, again, brightly colored ones will chance dyes and inks being transferred to the food, so it is best to get pure white.

Homemade pottery can also present a problem. There is a chance the pottery can be painted with a leaded glaze, and thus the microwaves will not be able to penetrate the surface and the food will not be able to cook. Further, leaded glazes are not recommended for eating utensils. If in doubt, do not use it.

WHAT DOES IT MEAN IN A RECIPE WHEN IT SAYS TO STIR THE FOOD OR TURN THE DISH? IS THAT THE SAME THING?

Stirring and turning are two different manoeuvers. Stirring is putting a utensil into a liquidy mixture and mixing the mixture. Because microwaves cook from the outside to the center of the food, the food just inside the edges of the dish will be hottest while the food in the centre will be slightly cooler. By stirring, you combine the hotter mixture with the cooler mixture for a more even cooking process. If you were away from the oven and were unable to stir the food, it would still cook, but it would take longer and would not cook quite so evenly. Turning, however is another matter. To turn the dish you must physically lift it and turn it 90 degrees. When microwave ovens first appeared on the market years ago, some of them were not designed to provide even cooking because of uneven distribution of the microwaves, thus creating "hot spots" or areas within the oven that received more microwaves and thus cooked food in that area of the oven quicker. With new technology and improved microwave distribution, uneven cooking and major hot spots have been virtually eliminated. However, when cooking something like lasagne or a cake for example, where the batter or mixture cannot be stirred to allow the core food to mingle with the outer edged mass, by turning the dish, you are in effect allowing the microwaves to hit any particular point in the casserole or dish at a different angle, thus again, allowing for more even cooking.

Undoubtedly, food in the microwave sometimes takes a little more attention than that cooked in a conventional oven, but in the over-all savings of time and energy and electrical consumption, the extra bit of attention you may have to give is well worth the effort.

CAN YOU USE ALUMINUM FOIL IN THE MICROWAVE OVEN, AND WHAT IS "SHIELDING"?

Shielding is the use of aluminum foil in the oven to prevent microwaves from penetrating into food. Microwaves cannot pass through metal and by covering parts of food with foil we can prevent them from cooking. An example would be covering the tips of the wings of a chicken or turkey. Because there is little to cook in this particular area it is quite likely that it would overcook. By covering it with foil the microwaves cannot get at the area and the cooking process is halted. Two important rules when using foil in the microwave are: there must be more food than foil; and the foil must not touch the walls, floor or ceiling of the microwave oven.

WHAT DO FP AND PL7 MEAN?

Variable power settings on the microwave oven allow us to cook foods at a rate suitable to their density. For example, it takes far less energy (lower power setting, but more time) to cook a roast of beef than it does to reheat a muffin. By adjusting the power setting we can tailor the amount of energy used to the amount of energy needed to get the job done. For recipes in this book we refer to the highest setting on your microwave oven as "FULL POWER", or 100%, or scaled one to ten, ten. Therefore "HALF POWER" is referred to as 50% or Power Level 5 (PL5). "LOW POWER" is referred to as 10% or Power Level 1 (PL1). In between, "MEDIUM HIGH" is 70% or Power Level 7 (PL7) and "MEDIUM LOW" is 30% or Power Level 3 (PL3). The term microwave has been shortened to MW, so an instruction reading Microwave Full Power for 30 seconds will read MW FP 30 seconds.

WHY DO RECIPES CALL FOR 2 TO 4 MINUTES INSTEAD OF A SPECIFIC AMOUNT OF TIME?

Timing is important when using your microwave oven. The more food you put into the oven, the longer it will take to cook. Wattages vary in different sizes and brands of microwave ovens and all the recipes in this book were timed using a 650 to 700 watt oven, so times may have to be adjusted according to the wattage of your particular oven. Times given are a guideline, and keep in mind, it is always better to undercook and add time than to try to revive something that is overcooked. With regards to output of wattage, be sure that the microwave is on its own circuit. If it were on the same circuit as another appliance, say for example the refrigerator, whenever the oven is operating and the fridge cuts on, the amount of power going to the microwave will be decreased, thus not allowing it to produce to its fullest capacity and increasing the time it takes to cook foods.

(IF I EAT SOMETHING AS SOON AS I TAKE IT OUT OF THE MICROWAVE OVEN, WILL I BE EATING MICROWAVES?)

The answer is NO. If you took a roast from a conventional oven and ate it right away would you be eating electricity? Of course not! But the fact that the heat that is within the food is continuing to cook it, brings out the importance of standing time for foods cooked in the microwave. So if a recipe calls for standing time, be sure to take it into account as part of the time you will need to cook the food. The food does not have to stand in the microwave, but should generally be covered during the standing time. Make use of this time to prepare other parts of the meal using your microwave oven.

HOW CAN I CLEAN MY MY MICROWAVE OVEN?

Never use abrasive cleansers or ammonia based cleansers in the microwave. Abrasive cleansers will permanently scratch the surface of the oven and ammonia based cleaners can leave an ammonia residue on the oven surface which can later evaporate into foods being heated in the oven.

The best method I have found to clean the oven is to soak a cloth or sponge with warm water. Place in the microwave oven and MW FP for three to five minutes. Carefully remove the hot, wet sponge using rubber gloves and then simply wipe the oven clean with a second cloth or sponge. If food particles remain stuck in the oven, simply repeat the steaming process, or throw away the oven - just kidding!

It is a good idea to keep ahead of spills and just wipe the oven clean on a regular basis, particularly around the door locking devices and around the door seal.

BEATING THE HEAT WAVE

1	lb. of delicious recipes	1	pinch of blessings from
1	ton of energy	10	years of experience
1	wealth of knowledge	5	handfuls of contributions

Mix ingredients. Spice it up with some humor. Microwave full power until flavors are developed. Nurture full steam ahead until hot off the press. Delicious, delightful and a sure success.

APPETIZERS

ARTICHOKE SQUARES

6   oz. jar marinated artichoke hearts, drained and chopped
4   eggs, beaten
1   tsp. garlic salt
½   tsp. salt
¼   tsp. pepper
3   tbsp. instant onion
¼   c. bread crumbs
⅛   tsp. Tabasco sauce
⅛   tsp. oregano
1¼ c. grated Cheddar cheese
    Parsley, chopped

Mix all ingredients except grated cheese and parsley and pour into a buttered 8 x 8 inch microproof dish. Place pan in a larger pan of hot water. Do not cover. MW FP for 7 minutes, rotating after each minute. Sprinkle with grated Cheddar cheese and chopped parsley. MW FP 1 minute. Cool and refrigerate. Cut into one inch squares. Can be served cold, or reheat if you wish.

AUNTY JUDY'S JUMPIN' JACK LUNCH IN A FLASH

Known for her quick wit, choice of the finer things in life and no fooling around in the kitchen Aunty Judy, Judy, Judy give us this quickie . . .

A handful or two of plain tortilla chips

A handful or two of shredded Monterey Jack cheese

Sprinkle chips with shredded cheese, MW FP until cheese is bubbly, a minute or two. Serve with refried beans and taco sauce. If you find the cheese is too "tough" for your liking, try using PL6.

CHEESE AND SAUSAGE APPETIZERS WITH MUSTARD SAUCE

¾   c. Bisquick
4   oz. Cheddar cheese (1 cup grated)
1   lb. pork sausage meat
1   egg, lightly beaten
½   tsp. salt
¼   tsp. pepper
    Dash garlic powder
¼   c. bread crumbs
1   tsp. oregano or Italian seasoning
    Mustard Sauce
    (see page 8)

Combine Bisquick and cheese. Mix in egg, sausage, salt, pepper and garlic powder. Shape mixture into 36 balls. Combine bread crumbs with oregano. Roll each ball in crumb mixture. Set 12 balls on a plate and MW FP 2 minutes. Balls should spring to the touch when done. Serve hot with Mustard Sauce.

MUSTARD SAUCE

2 eggs, slightly beaten	¼ c. milk
¼ c. white sugar	¼ c. white vinegar
2 - 3 tsp. dry mustard	2 tbsp. butter or margarine

Put ingredients into a 2 cup measure. Whisk. MW FP 2 minutes, whisking several times after the first minute until the mixture comes to the boil and is thickened. Stir often. If you overcook this mixture it will curdle and you will have scrambled eggs. You just want to thicken it, so watch it carefully.

CHEESE PUFFS

1 c. grated sharp Cheddar cheese	1 tsp. garlic salt
1 tbsp. flour	1 tbsp. dry white wine
1 tsp. curry powder	2 egg whites
	12 crackers

In small bowl, combine cheese, flour, curry, garlic salt and wine. Beat egg whites until stiff; fold into first mixture. Drop by teaspoons on wax paper. Place each cheese puff on cracker on microproof serving dish. MW FP 1-1½ minutes for 12 crackers, rotating dish ¼ turn halfway through cooking, until cheese begins to bubble. Serve while hot. YIELD: 10 - 12 servings.

Cheese mixture can be shaped around a green olive for an interesting variation. Serve with colorful cheese and cracker arrangement and deviled eggs.

CHRISTMAS TREE DIP

1 tbsp. butter	8 oz. cream cheese
3 tbsp. white vinegar	Few drops Tabasco sauce
3 tbsp. white sugar	1 red pepper, finely diced
3 eggs, slightly beaten	1 green pepper, finely diced
1 c. chopped green onion	

Put butter in a 2 cup measure and MW FP 30 seconds or until melted. Whisk in vinegar, sugar and eggs. MW FP 1 to 2 minutes, whisking every 15 seconds. Mixture should be thickened, but do not overcook or it will curdle. Cut cream cheese into chunks and drop into hot egg mixture and whisk until cream cheese is melted. Add Tabasco sauce, onion and peppers. Chill. Serve with raw vegetables.

HINT:

— *Soften dried fruit by sprinkling with water and MW FP 1 - 2 minutes in a covered container.*

CHICKEN KABOBS

This recipe is tried and true. The thing that Vera makes for dinner most often is a reservation, so when she gives you a recipe you know it has to be quick and easy. Thanks Vera.

1	lb. boned chicken breasts, skinned and cut into 1-inch cubes	⅛	tsp. ground ginger
			Dash pepper
¼	c. soya sauce	1	green pepper, cut into ½-inch cubes
2	tsp. sugar	4	oz. mushrooms (about 15 med. mushrooms), halved
½	tsp. salt		
⅛	tsp. garlic powder	2	tbsp. honey

Mix chicken pieces, soya sauce, sugar, salt, garlic powder, ginger and pepper. Let stand 10 to 20 minutes. Drain, reserving soya sauce mixture.

Alternate 1 green pepper cube, 1 chicken cube and 1 mushroom half on round wooden toothpicks. Place kabobs on single layer of paper toweling in a spoke pattern on roasting rack. Stir honey into reserved soya sauce mixture; brush each kabob generously.

MW FP until chicken is tender and green peppers are tender-crisp, 3½ to 6½ minutes, brushing each kabob with soya sauce mixture after half the cooking time. Rotate after half the cooking time.

Variation: Substitute 15 oz. can pineapple chunks (juice pack), drained, for mushrooms. YIELD: 30 kabobs.

CRAB CANAPES

	Baked hors d'oeuvres size tart shells, or cherry tomatoes with tops cut off & seeded, or toast rounds	2	tbsp. finely diced onion
		1	tbsp. parsley flakes
		1	tsp. chili sauce
6	oz. crab seafood sticks	½	tsp. Worcestershire sauce
½	c. mayonnaise	1 - 2	drops Tabasco sauce
¼	c. grated Cheddar cheese		Salt to taste
		4	oz. cream cheese (garnish)

Chop seafood sticks finely and combine with remaining ingredients EXCEPT CREAM CHEESE. Mix well. Heap mixture into tart shells, tomatoes or onto toast rounds. Line oven with paper towels. Put half of the canapes on toweling in a ring pattern and MW PL7 1½ - 2 minutes or until cheese is melted. Soften cream cheese and put into a piping bag fitted with a star tip. Put a cream cheese rosette on each canape. Serve hot.

HINT:

— **Make extra waffles or pancakes and freeze. Reheat as needed on PL4.**

CURRIED CRAB TARTS

1 tbsp. minced onion	1 c. crab meat or crab
2 tbsp. butter	flavored sea sticks
1 tbsp. flour	Grated cheese
1 tsp. curry powder	Paprika
¼ tsp. salt	20 small baked tart shells
½ c. light cream	

Put butter and onion in a microproof bowl. MW FP 1½ to 2 minutes until onion is transparent. Whisk in flour and seasonings. Whisk in cream. MW FP for 3 minutes. Stir. Add crab. Spoon into baked tart shells. Sprinkle with grated cheese and sprinkle with paprika. Set tartlettes in a ring pattern on a serving plate. MW FP until hot and cheese is melted.

HAM NUGGET SNACKS

1 can Pillsbury refrigerator biscuits	½ tsp. chili powder
	8 oz. cooked ham
⅓ c. toasted bread crumbs	4 oz. Cheddar cheese
2 tbsp. grated Parmesan cheese	(1 cup grated)
	1 tbsp. mustard
¼ c. melted butter or margarine	¼ c. sweet relish

Open biscuit dough and lay out on waxed paper. Press cut lines together to get one long strip of dough. Using a sharp knife, cut into 24 even squares. Cover with waxed paper and set aside while preparing coating and filling. In a bowl mix together bread crumbs, Parmesan cheese and chili powder. Set aside. To make filling chop ham very fine or use food processor to chop. Add grated Cheddar cheese, mustard and relish and mix well. Put a spoonful of filling mixture on each square of dough. Bring points together and pinch to make sealed "nuggets". Dip each nugget in melted margarine and then roll in crumb mixture. Cook in two batches, placing nuggets in a ring pattern on platter. MW FP 3 to 5 minutes. Dough will spring to the touch when done.

HOT ROQUEFORT DIP

8 oz. cream cheese	1 tbsp. finely minced onion
½ c. crumbled Roquefort cheese (about 2 oz.)	1 tsp. horseradish
	½ tsp. Worcestershire sauce
3 tbsp. milk	¼ c. finely chopped walnuts
1 tbsp. dried parsley flakes	

Combine all ingredients except chopped walnuts in small bowl. MW PL5 until heated through, 3 to 5 minutes, stirring after half the cooking time. Sprinkle with walnuts. Serve with snack crackers or raw vegetables. YIELD: 1½ cups.

LEMONY COCKTAIL SAUSAGES

2 lb. cocktail sausages,   ¼ c. sherry
   individually cut   1 clove garlic, minced
1 c. chili sauce   Grated rind of ½ lemon

Brown sausages on conventional range top in frying pan. Put in 8 x 8 inch microproof dish.

Mix together chili sauce, sherry, garlic and lemon rind. Pour chili sauce mixture over sausages. Cover. MW FP 5 minutes, stirring once or twice. Cool. Let stand in refrigerator overnight. MW FP, uncovered, 2 minutes or until hot. Serve with cocktail picks. YIELD: approx. 6 dozen appetizers.

MEXICAN LASAGNE

¼ c. chopped onion   ¼ tsp. ground cumin
¼ c. chopped green pepper   ⅛ tsp. pepper
¼ c. chopped sweet red   4 c. broken tortilla chips
   pepper   1½ c. shredded Monterey
4 eggs   Jack cheese
1 c. creamed cottage cheese   1½ c. shredded Cheddar
½ tsp. salt   cheese
½ tsp. oregano   1 c. sour cream

half Mix together eggs, cottage cheese and seasonings. Sprinkle 1½ cups chips over bottom of 12 x 8 inch casserole dish. Spoon of cottage cheese mixture over chips. Combine onion, green and red peppers, and spread half of onion mixture over cottage cheese. Sprinkle 1 cup Monterey Jack and 1 cup Cheddar cheese. Repeat, chips, cottage cheese and onion layers, retaining ½ cup chips for topping.

MW FP 5 minutes. MW PL5 for 9 - 14 minutes or until centre is set. Rotate dish after half the cooking time. Combine remaining cheeses and sour cream. Spread over casserole. Sprinkle with remaining chips. MW FP 3 - 5 minutes, rotating dish after half the cooking time. Let stand 3 minutes before serving. YIELD: 9 servings.

HINTS:

— *Perk one large pot of coffee. Remove the grounds and reheat by the cup as needed. The coffee won't become bitter as it does when kept warm all day long.*

— *To dry stale bread for croutons or crumbs MW FP 6 to 7 minutes (4 cups of bread cubes).*

MINI PIZZAS

English muffins
Barbecue sauce
Grated Mozzarella cheese
Salami slices
Sliced mushrooms
Anything but the kitchen sink

Cut open 2 muffins. Spread each piece with barbecue sauce. Place 2 slices of salami on each. Add mushrooms, sliced olives, chopped green pepper, or whatever you like. Cover each piece with grated cheese. Put a paper towel on the MW oven floor, put pizzas on paper towel, MW 60% for 2 minutes. *If you microwave cheese at too high a power level it will get tough and rubbery.

NUTS AND BOLTS

¾ c. margarine or butter
2 tbsp. Worcestershire sauce
1½ tsp. celery salt
1 tsp. onion powder
1 tsp. garlic powder
2½ c. bite-sized shredded wheat squares
4 c. toasted "o" cereal
1½ c. salted nuts
2 c. thin pretzel sticks

Combine margarine, Worcestershire sauce and spices in small bowl. MW FP until margarine melts, 1 to 2 minutes. Stir to blend.

Combine remaining ingredients in 3-quart casserole. Add margarine mixture, tossing to blend. MW FP until cereal is well coated and crisp, 5 to 6 minutes, stirring every minute. Spread evenly onto paper toweling-lined tray or cookie sheet. Cool. YIELD: 8 cups.

SHRIMP MOLD

1 can tomato soup
8 oz. pkg. cream cheese, cubed
1 env. Knox gelatine
2 cans shrimp, drained or 1 small pkg. frozen shrimp, thawed
1 c. mayonnaise
½ c. chopped celery
½ c. chopped green pepper
½ c. chopped onion
¼ c. cold water
Dash garlic salt
Salt and pepper
1 tbsp. lemon juice
2 - 3 tbsp. horseradish

Put soup and cream cheese in a bowl. MW FP 2 to 4 minutes, stirring every minute, until hot and well blended. Soak gelatine in water and add cheese and soup mixture. Cool 30 minutes. Add remaining ingredients and pour into 1-quart oiled mold. Serve with snack crackers, etc.

PINEAPPLE RUMAKI

20 oz. tin pineapple chunks in juice	½ tsp. ground cloves
1 lb. fresh chicken livers	½ tsp. dried mustard
2 tbsp. brown sugar, packed	1½ lb. sliced bacon (about 40 slices)

Drain pineapple very well (reserve juice for another use). Trim livers and cut each in half. If some halves are too large, cut in half again. You should have about 30 pieces of liver.

Arrange drained pineapple and liver pieces on large tray or board in single layer.

In small cup or bowl, mix together brown sugar, cloves and mustard using fingers. Sprinkle mixture evenly over pineapple and livers and let stand.

Meanwhile, on microwave bacon rack or plate, place 6 - 8 strips of bacon at a time in single layer. Cover with waxed paper and MW FP for 4 minutes.

Strips should begin to look slightly brown, losing their transluscence, but not crisp. If necessary, rotate rack half turn after 1½ minutes or rearrange strips for most even cooking. Repeat until all bacon is partially cooked. Drain grease as needed.

When bacon is cool enough to handle, place one pineapple chunk and one liver piece at one end of a bacon strip and roll to enclose in bacon. With wooden toothpick, firmly skewer roll, catching exposed end of bacon slice, pineapple and liver piece.

Arrange about 12 rumaki in circle on microwave trivet and cover with waxed paper. MW FP for 5 to 7 minutes. Large rolls might need an additional few seconds. Repeat until all rumaki are cooked. Serve hot. YIELD: about 50 pieces.

SPINACH APPETIZERS

1 lge. onion, chopped finely	¼ c. Parmesan cheese
½ c. butter or margarine	1 tsp. seasoned salt
10 oz. pkg. frozen spinach	½ tsp. garlic salt
1 c. herb-seasoned stuffing mix (crumb type, not cubes)	¼ tsp. thyme
	¼ tsp. pepper
	3 eggs

Combine onion and butter in a 2-quart bowl. MW FP 3 - 4 minutes, uncovered, or until onion is tender, stirring once. Set aside. Leaving spinach in package, MW FP 3 - 4 minutes or until thawed. Open one end of package and squeeze to drain liquid. Add spinach to onion mixture. Stir in remaining ingredients, mixing well. Refrigerate until chilled, about 1 hour. Shape teaspoons of mixture into 1-inch balls. Arrange on 2 serving platters. For each plate MW FP 4 - 5 minutes, uncovered, or until appetizers are set.

STUFFED MUSHROOMS (ALMOND & SHERRY)

1	lb. lge. fresh mushrooms	1	tbsp. parsley flakes
1	tbsp. butter or margarine, melted	⅛	tsp. pepper
		½	tsp. salt
¾	c. finely chopped green onions (whites & greens)	¼	tsp. marjoram
		¼	tsp. thyme
3	slices crustless bread, torn in tiny pieces	1	tsp. Worcestershire sauce
		3	tbsp. sherry
¼	c. toasted & chopped slivered almonds	1	egg, slightly beaten

Wash mushrooms, remove stems and pat dry. Place caps in a ring pattern on a baking dish. Chop mushroom stems and add with butter and onions to a microproof dish. MW FP for 3 minutes. Add remaining ingredients. Fill mushroom caps. MW FP 3 minutes until just tender. If you overcook the mushroom caps they will be watery and limp.

STUFFED MUSHROOMS (BACON & CHEDDAR)

8	oz. fresh mushrooms (about 12 - 1½-inch mushrooms)	⅓	cup finely chopped green onions
		½	tsp. salt
3	slices bacon, chopped	¼	tsp. pepper

2 - 4	drops Tabasco sauce	2	tbsp. shredded Cheddar cheese
1	tbsp. all-purpose flour		
¼	c. whipping cream		

Wash mushrooms. Remove stems and chop fine. Place mushroom caps on paper toweling on dinner plate. MW PL7 1 minute. Drain and set aside. Place bacon in medium bowl. MW FP until crisp, 2½ - 3 minutes. Drain. Add chopped mushroom stems, onions, salt, pepper and Tabasco sauce. MW FP until mushrooms and onions are tender, 2 - 3½ minutes.

Blend in flour; stir in cream until smooth. MW PL7 until thickened and smooth, 2 - 3 minutes, stirring once or twice during cooking. Stir in cheese.

Fill each mushroom cap with bacon mixture. Place around outer edge of 9-inch pie plate or dinner plate. MW FP until cheese melts, 1 - 1½ minutes. Rotate plate half turn after half the cooking time. YIELD: approx. 12 appetizers.

HINT:

— *Soften hardened brown sugar by adding a slice of apple or bread and MW FP 1 minute in a covered container. Or put sugar in oven with 1 cup hot water and MW FP 2 - 3 minutes/lb.*

STUFFED MUSHROOMS (CREAM CHEESE)

Several large firm		6	tbsp. Parmesan cheese
mushrooms		¼	tsp. garlic powder
1 - 8 oz. pkg. cream cheese			(or more to taste)
¼	c. sour cream		

Wash mushrooms and remove stems. Chop stems very fine. Mix cheeses and sour cream together and season. Add chopped stems. Stuff ingredients into mushroom caps. Place on plate in a circular pattern. MW FP until warmed through. Serve warm.

STUFFED MUSHROOMS (MY FAVORITE)

My son Kyle has contributed to the levity in this cook book. Heaven knows we all need a rise out of cooking other than from the yeast, so, send your groans to him!

Enter the prodigal son - stage left. *"Hi Mom! What's the smallest room in the world?"* O.K., I'll bite Kyle, what's the smallest room in the world? *"A MUSHROOM!!"* Cute Kyle, really cute! Well, there's more than one way to fill the smallest room in the world, other than inviting 30 gnomes in for cocktails, and here's my favorite.

24	mushrooms	¼	tsp. salt
1	tbsp. margarine or butter	⅛	tsp. pepper
3	green onions	1	c. grated Mozzarella
¼	lb. spicy salami		cheese

Clean mushrooms. Carefully remove stems. Chop stems finely - a food processor is great for this job. Chop green onions finely. Put margarine or butter into a pie plate and MW FP 45 seconds to melt. Add chopped mushroom stems and chopped onions; MW FP 2 minutes to saute gently. Stir 2 or 3 times during cooking. Chop salami finely; again, the food processor is a great help. Mix with mushroom mixture. Add grated cheese to the mushroom mixture. Spoon mixture into mushroom caps. (I use a baby's feeding spoon, it's just the right size.) Set the mushrooms on a serving plate arranged in a ring pattern doing about 12 mushrooms at a time. MW FP until thoroughly heated and the cheese is melted. Any extra filling can be heated and served on crackers.

HINT:
— *To bring cheese to room temperature for fuller flavor, MW PL2 - 1 minute.*

TACO DIP

1½ - 2 lb. ground beef	½ c. Parmesan cheese
2 tbsp. vegetable oil	8 oz. tomato sauce
½ c. chopped onion	1 c. taco sauce
1 tsp. oregano	8 oz. cream cheese
Dash salt	

Crumble ground beef into microproof colander. Set over casserole. MW FP 8 - 10 minutes or until no longer pink. Discard fat. Put oil and onion in casserole. MW FP 3 - 4 minutes or until transparent. Mix in cooked beef and balance of ingredients. MW FP 3 to 5 minutes, stirring after every minute until thoroughly heated and cream cheese is melted. Serve with corn chips.

TUNA TREATS

6 oz. can tuna	¼ c. mayonnaise
1 egg, beaten	2 tbsp. chopped parsley
¼ c. chopped onion	1 tbsp. mustard (paste)
1 c. bread crumbs	1 tsp. fine herb seasoning
½ - 10½ oz. can consomme	1 c. crushed crackers
(concentrated)	

Break tuna into pieces. Combine tuna with beaten egg, chopped onion, bread crumbs, consomme, mayonnaise, parsley, mustard and fine herb seasoning. Refrigerate mixture 15 minutes. Shape the mixture into balls. Roll balls in cracker crumbs. Place the balls on a plate. MW FP 3 minutes. Serve with Hollandaise Sauce (see page 38) or Mustard Sauce (see page 10). YIELD: 6 servings.

HINTS:

— *To soften hard ice cream for easy scooping, MW PL3 14 seconds/pint.*

— *To blanch almonds or other nuts, put in casserole, cover with hot water, cover casserole and MW FP 1 minute. Rinse in cold water.*

— *To extract more juice from citrus fruits MW FP 20 to 30 seconds before using.*

CHICKEN BROTH

3	lb. frying chicken	¼	tsp. thyme
1	c. chopped onion	5	whole peppercorns
1	c. thinly sliced celery	2	cloves garlic
1	c. thinly sliced carrots	1	bay leaf
½	c. snipped fresh parsley	2	whole cloves
2	tsp. salt	8	c. water
1	tbsp. fresh dill weed		

Put chicken in a 5-quart casserole. Add remaining ingredients. Cover. MW FP 35 - 45 minutes until vegetables are tender and chicken is no longer pink. Remove chicken from broth. Remove meat from bones. Cut up and use as desired. Strain broth through cheesecloth-lined colander. Freezes well.

CHUNKY BEEF SOUP

1	lb. beef chuck cut into ½-inch cubes	1	c. diced potato (not too fine)
1	c. chopped onion	½	c. snipped fresh parsley
1	c. diced celery (not too fine)	2	tsp. salt
1	c. diced carrot (not too fine)	5	whole peppercorns
		2	cloves garlic
		8	c. water

Put ingredients into a 5-quart casserole. Cover. MW FP 40 to 45 minutes until beef is tender.

CHICKEN NOODLE SOUP

6	c. chicken broth	1	tbsp. white wine
2½	c. cubed cooked chicken	½	tsp. salt
½	c. narrow egg noodles	¼	tsp. dried summer savory leaves
¼	c. diced carrot		
2	tbsp. fresh snipped parsley		

Combine ingredients in a 3-quart casserole. Cover and MW FP 20 - 25 minutes, stirring every 5 minutes, until carrots and noodles are tender.

CREAM OF CHICKEN SOUP

2	tbsp. butter	¼	c. diced carrot
¼	c. all-purpose flour	2	tbsp. fresh snipped parsley
4	c. chicken broth	1	tbsp. white wine
2	c. light cream	½	tsp. salt
¼	tsp. ground turmeric		

Put butter in 3-quart casserole. MW FP 45 seconds or until melted. Stir in flour. Blend in broth, cream and turmeric. Add balance of ingredients. MW FP 20 to 25 minutes, stirring every 5 minutes until hot. Do not boil.

SPLIT PEA SOUP

6	c. water	3	med. carrots,
1	lb. dried green split peas		coarsely grated
	(about 2½ cups)	1½	tsp. salt
1	med. onion, thinly sliced	¼	tsp. pepper

Combine all ingredients in 3-quart casserole; cover. MW FP 10 minutes. MW PL5 until vegetables are tender and soup is thickened, 1 hour - 1 hour 10 minutes, stirring 2 - 3 times during cooking. YIELD: 8 servings.

CREAM OF MUSHROOM SOUP

¼	c. butter or margarine	½	tsp. salt
2	tbsp. finely chopped onion		Dash pepper
1	c. thinly sliced fresh	2	c. chicken broth
	mushrooms	1½	c. light cream
⅓	c. all-purpose flour	1	tbsp. snipped fresh parsley

In 2-quart casserole combine butter, onion and mushrooms. MW FP 3 - 5 minutes or until onion and mushrooms are tender, stirring every minute. Stir in flour, salt and pepper. Blend in broth, cream and parsley. MW FP 9 - 12 minutes, or until mixture thickens, stirring with wire whisk every 2 minutes. YIELD: 4 servings.

VARIATIONS:

CREAM OF BROCCOLI SOUP

Follow recipe above, substituting 1½ cups finely chopped broccoli flowerets for mushrooms. Garnish with thin lemon slice, if desired.

CREAM OF CARROT SOUP

Follow recipe above, substituting 1½ cups grated carrots for mushrooms. Garnish each serving with a dollop of dairy sour cream and a dash of ground cinnamon, if desired.

GROUND BEEF SOUP

1	lb. lean ground beef	1	tsp. salt
1	c. chopped onion	½	tsp. dried basil leaves
1	c. chopped celery	¼	tsp. pepper
4	c. hot water	1	bay leaf
2	c. ½-inch potato cubes	3	tomatoes, cut into eighths
1	c. thinly sliced carrots		& sliced in half

Mix ground beef, onion and celery in 5-quart casserole. MW FP until ground beef loses its pink color, 5 - 7 minutes, stirring after half the cooking time.

Add hot water, potatoes, carrots, salt, basil, pepper and bay leaf; cover. MW FP until potatoes are tender, 18 - 20 minutes.

Add tomatoes. MW FP until tomatoes are tender, 8 - 10 minutes. YIELD: 8 servings.

NEW ENGLAND CLAM CHOWDER

3   slices bacon, chopped
2 - 6½ oz. cans minced
     clams, drained
     (reserve ⅓ cup liquid)
1 ½ c. ½-inch potato cubes
½   c. chopped onion

3   tbsp. all-purpose flour
1½ c. milk
1   tsp. salt
⅛   tsp. pepper
1   c. light cream

Place bacon in 2-quart casserole. MW FP until bacon is crisp, 3 - 4 minutes. Add reserved clam juice, potatoes and onion. Cover. MW FP until potatoes are tender, 8 - 10 minutes, stirring after half the cooking time.

Blend in flour. Stir in milk, salt and pepper. MW FP until thickened, 5 - 7 minutes, stirring after half the cooking time. Stir 2 or 3 times during cooking.

Blend in cream, stir in clams. MW PL7 until thickened and heated through, 4 - 5 minutes. YIELD: 4 servings.

HINT:

— *Dry fresh herbs between paper towels. Rinse, shake off excess moisture. Separate the leaves from stems. Spread 1 cup of leaves on a double thickness of paper towel and MW FP 2 - 3 minutes or until the leaves are brittle. Let stand 10 - 15 minutes. Crush and store in airtight container.*

ONION SOUP

¼   c. margarine or butter
2   med. onions, thinly sliced
4   c. hot water
1⅜ oz. pkg. onion soup mix
2   tsp. instant beef bouillon

1   tsp. Worcestershire sauce
4 - ½-inch slices toasted
     French bread
¼   c. grated Parmesan cheese

Combine margarine and onion in 2-quart casserole. MW FP until onions are tender-crisp, 4 - 6 minutes.

Add water, onion soup mix, instant bouillon and Worcestershire sauce; cover. MW FP 5 minutes. MW PL5 until onions are tender and flavors are blended, 15 -20 minutes.

Ladle soup into 4 individual serving bowls. Place toast on top. Sprinkle each with 1 tablespoon Parmesan cheese. MW FP until cheese softens, 5 - 7 minutes. YIELD: 4 servings.

SEASONED CROUTONS

2 c. bread cubes	¼ tsp. garlic salt
2 - 3 tsp. seasoning salt	3 tbsp. melted butter

Place bread cubes in baking pan. MW FP 2 - 2½ minutes. Stir part way through time. (Cubes will begin to dry.) Sprinkle seasoning over bread cubes evenly. Drizzle butter, tossing to coat. MW FP 1 - 2 minutes, stirring after each minute, until dry and crisp.

TOMATO BREW

10¾ oz. can condensed tomato soup	2 tbsp. finely chopped onion
16 oz. can tomatoes, undrained	¼ tsp. Worcestershire sauce
	⅛ tsp. dill (optional)
1 c. buttermilk	Seasoned Croutons

Combine all ingredients in a 2-quart glass casserole. Break up whole tomatoes with other ingredients; mix until buttermilk is completely blended into other liquid. Cover with lid or plastic wrap. MW on roast for 10 - 12 minutes, or until hot. Garnish with seasoned croutons, parsley or Parmesan cheese.

VEGETABLE SOUP

3 slices bacon, chopped	3 tbsp. all-purpose flour
1 c. chopped celery	3 c. vegetable juice cocktail
¼ c. chopped onion	2 c. water
2 c. ½-inch potato cubes	10 oz. pkg. frozen green peas
1 c. thinly sliced carrots	1 tsp. salt
¼ c. water	¼ tsp. pepper

Combine bacon, celery and onion in 5-quart casserole. MW FP until bacon is crisp and vegetables tender, 4 - 6 minutes.

Add potatoes, carrots and ¼ cup water; cover. MW FP until potatoes are tender, 12 - 15 minutes, stirring after half the cooking time.

Blend in flour. Stir in vegetable juice, 2 cups water, the green peas, salt and pepper. Cover. MW FP until soup is slightly thickened and peas are heated through, 8 - 10 minutes. Stir after half the cooking time. YIELD: 8 servings.

HINT:

— *Soften butter and cream cheese spreads so that they do not tear the bread when spreading. MW PL2 1 minute.*

EGGS

HOW TO COOK EGGS

Never cook eggs in the shell.

If cooking eggs "whole", i.e. not scrambled, be sure to pierce the yolk several times. This breaks the membrane covering the yolk. If the membrane is not broken steam can build up under the membrane causing an "explosion".

Use less butter when cooking eggs in the microwave. The flavor of the butter is amplified and because of the short cooking time there is little evaporation of the liquids in the butter and thus less butter is needed.

Always account for and make use of standing time when cooking eggs. Again, because they cook so quickly, it is very easy to overcook them. Eggs should appear moist at the end of the cooking time, and will continue to cook and lose the gloss during the standing time.

HINTS:
— *Warm damp cloths for finger towels in microwave.*
— *To warm pies or melt cheese on pie MW PL4 1 minute.*

ASPARAGUS & HAM QUICHE

1	can asparagus tips	½	tsp. salt
1	c. cubed ham	1	c. shredded Monterey Jack cheese
4	eggs		
¾	c. cream	1	c. shredded Cheddar cheese
¾	c. milk		
¼	c. chopped onion	1	pastry shell
⅛	tsp. cayenne pepper		

Line cooked pastry shell with asparagus, onion, ham and cheese. Beat eggs, and blend together with milk, cream, salt, cayenne. Pour over cheese mixture. Garnish with paprika.

MW FP 10 minutes, rotating twice. Quiche is cooked when it is set but still jiggles slightly when shaken. Cover. Let stand 5 - 10 minutes before serving. YIELD: 6 servings.

SCRAMBLED EGGS

2	tsp. butter	2	eggs
2	tsp. milk		

Place butter in glass measuring cup or custard dish. MW FP 30 seconds or until melted. Add eggs and milk, and beat until well blended. MW FP 1 - 1½ minutes. Stir set portions from the outside to the centre. When done eggs should be just past runny stage. Let stand 1 - 2 minutes.

BAKED EGGS IN BOLOGNA CUPS

4   slices bologna   Salt & pepper to taste
4   eggs

For each serving, line 6-ounce custard cup with bologna. Break egg into centre. Season with salt and pepper. With toothpick, pierce egg yolk twice and egg white several times.

Cover each cup with plastic wrap. MW PL5 2 - 3 minutes. Let stand, covered, 2 minutes before serving. YIELD: 4 servings.

NOTE: For 2 baked eggs follow above procedure, halve all ingredients. MW PL5 1¼ - 1¾ minutes. Let stand 1 minute.

CHEESE BAKE

1   slice bread   ⅓   c. milk
½   c. grated cheese (Swiss, 2   slices of bacon
     Cheddar or Mozzarella)   Sprinkle of salt
1   egg   Sprinkle of pepper

Put bacon on a plate. Cover with a waxed paper. MW FP 2 - 3 minutes. Let stand 3 minutes. While bacon is cooking and standing, grate cheese. Put the slice of bread in a glass or MW pie plate. Sprinkle with cheese. Measure milk into a 1-cup measuring cup. Add the egg and whisk with a whisk or fork.

Crumble the bacon, which is cool enough to handle by now, into the milk/egg mixture. Add a sprinkle of salt and a sprinkle of pepper. Pour over the bread/cheese. Cover with plastic wrap, folding back one edge making a spot for the extra steam to escape. MW PL5 for 2½ - 3 minutes. Let stand 3 minutes. YIELD: 1 serving.

SWEET AND SOUR SAUCE

(for Chinese Omelette - Page 23)

2   tbsp. sugar   1   chicken bouillon cube
1   tbsp. tapioca starch   dissolved in —
1   tbsp. soya sauce   1   c. boiling water
1   tbsp. vinegar

In a 2-cup glass measure stir together sugar and tapioca starch. Add soya sauce and vinegar, stirring thoroughly. Stir in bouillon. MW FP 2½ - 3 minutes, uncovered, stirring after 1 minute and again at the end of cooking time. Sauce should have boiled and thickened by end of cooking time, if not, MW for a few more seconds.

CHINESE OMELETTE

1 tbsp. butter	¾ c. fresh bean sprouts
¾ c. thinly sliced onion	4 eggs
¾ c. thinly sliced mushrooms	½ tsp. salt
¾ c. thinly sliced celery	⅛ tsp. pepper
(cut on 45 degree angle)	

Prepare Sweet and Sour Sauce (see page 22) and set aside.

In a 9-inch pie plate MW butter FP 25 - 30 seconds until melted. Stir in onion, mushrooms and celery. MW FP 2½ - 3½ minutes. Rinse and drain bean sprouts and stir into vegetables. Let cool slightly and drain off any excess liquid.

Beat together eggs, salt and pepper. Pour over vegetables in pie plate. MW FP 3½ - 5 minutes, uncovered. Stir twice during cooking, smoothing top of mixture with the back of a spoon.

At the end of the cooking time the omelette should appear glossy. Allow to stand 1 - 2 minutes. While omelette is standing reheat Sweet and Sour Sauce.

To serve, cut in wedges and top with sauce. Garnish with pineapple ring if desired.

HINT:

— *Warm bacon in package to separate slices easily.*

CREAMY EGGS

½ c. milk	1 lge. ripe tomato, diced
3 oz. pkg. cream cheese	Salt, pepper
6 med. eggs	2 tbsp. butter or margarine
1 c. diced cooked ham	

Place milk in 1-cup glass measure. MW FP 45 seconds.

Beat cream cheese until fluffy in large mixing bowl. Beat in milk and eggs. Stir in ham and tomato. Season with salt and pepper as desired.

Place butter in 10-inch pie plate. MW FP for 20 - 30 seconds or until melted. Pour egg mixture into pie plate, MW FP, covered, 8 - 10 minutes, or until firm, but moist. Stir 2 - 3 times during cooking time. YIELD: 4 servings.

HINTS: *(Making the most of your Microwave)*

— *Toast almonds.*

— *To heat ¼ cup brandy for flambeing MW FP 15 seconds.*

CRUSTLESS QUICHE LORRAINE

¾ c. chopped onion
1 c. grated Swiss cheese
4 eggs
⅛ tsp. cayenne

10 slices crisp cooked bacon
1 can (1 lb.) evaporated milk
¾ tsp. salt

Sprinkle onion into bottom of 9-inch pie plate. MW FP 2½ minutes to soften. Sprinkle bacon over onion. Sprinkle cheese over bacon. Pour milk into a 4 cup measure and MW FP 3 minutes. Beat eggs, salt and cayenne in a bowl and slowly add hot milk while beating with a whip. Pour into pie plate. MW FP 7 minutes, stirring every 2 minutes, bringing cooked outer portions of egg to center of dish. Smooth with back of spoon. Let stand, covered, for 5 - 10 minutes.

EGGS BENEDICT

4 poached eggs
½ c. butter
½ c. whipping cream
4 egg yolks, beaten

½ tsp. salt
2 tbsp. lemon juice
2 toasted English muffins
4 slices ham, lightly fried

While eggs are standing prepare Hollandaise Sauce. Put butter in a 4 cup glass measure. MW FP 1 - 1½ minutes or until melted.

Whisk in remaining ingredients. Whisk well. MW FP 1 - 2 minutes, uncovered, whisking every 30 seconds. Sauce should be the consistency of mayonnaise. DO NOT OVERCOOK or the result will be scrambled eggs.

Place toasted English muffin on serving plate, top with ham. Using slotted spoon, remove egg from water; drain and slide on top of ham. Top with sauce. Serve at once. YIELD: 2 - 4 servings.

HINT:

— *To clarify butter MW PL7 until melted, then boil. Let stand for 1 minute. The milk solids will settle to the bottom. The golden liquid on top is the clarified butter which can be carefully poured off and used as needed.*

EGG MINI-PIZZA

½ tsp. butter or margarine   1 tbsp. ketchup or
1 egg   tomato sauce
1 tbsp. water   1 tbsp. grated cheese
⅛ tsp. salt   4-6 thin slices pepperoni
⅛ tsp. oregano

Add any other pizza ingredients you wish, such as minced onion, chopped mushrooms, chopped green pepper, crumbled cooked bacon.

Put butter in a 10-ounce custard cup. MW FP for 20 - 25 seconds or until melted. Add egg, water, salt and oregano. Beat lightly with fork to blend yolk and white. MW FP 30 - 45 seconds. Stir.

MW FP for 10 - 15 seconds. Top with ketchup or tomato sauce, grated cheese and pepperoni. MW FP for 10 - 15 seconds. Egg will not be completely cooked. Cover and let stand for 1 minute to allow cooking to complete. Slip egg from custard cup onto toast or plate. YIELD: 1 serving.

FLUFFY CHEESE OMELETTE

3 eggs, separated   2 tbsp. butter
⅓ c. mayonnaise   ½ c. finely shredded cheese
2 tbsp. water

In large mixing bowl, beat egg whites at highest speed of mixer, until soft peaks form. In a smaller bowl, using same beaters, beat yolks, mayonnaise, and water. Gently pour yolk mixture over beaten whites. Fold together carefully.

Put butter in a 9-inch pie plate. MW FP for 1 minute, swirl to coat dish. Carefully pour egg mixture into pie plate. MW PL5, 6 - 8 minutes. Sprinkle cheese over omelette. MW PL5, ½ - 1 minute, until cheese is slightly melted.

Run edge of spatula around sides and bottom of dish. Fold omelette in half. Gently slide onto serving plate. Serve. YIELD: 1 or 2 servings.

HINTS: *(Making the most of your Microwave)*
— **Warm pet food if kept in fridge.**
— **Soften frozen juice concentrate for easy mixing.**

HERBED CHEESE SOUFFLE

¼ c. butter or margarine	1 c. shredded Cheddar cheese
¼ c. flour	
1 tsp. salt	6 eggs, separated
Dash cayenne pepper	1 tbsp. parsley flakes
1½ c. light cream or	½ tsp. thyme leaves
evaporated milk	1 tsp. cream of tartar

Put butter in 1½-quart casserole, MW FP 1 minute, or until melted. Blend in flour, salt and pepper. With wire whisk blend in cream. MW FP 3½ - 6½ minutes, or until sauce is thick and smooth, whisking after 2 minutes and then every minute. Whisk in cheese and blend until melted.

In small bowl, beat egg yolks lightly. Whisk in a small amount of the hot sauce. Whisk the egg yolk mixture into remaining sauce, whisking constantly to avoid lumping. Add parsley and thyme. Set aside.

In 2-quart mixing bowl at highest speed of electric mixer, beat egg whites and cream of tartar until stiff peaks form. Gently fold cheese mixture into egg whites.

Pour mixture into 2-quart souffle dish. MW PL4 25 - 35 minutes, or until top is dry, rotating dish 3 or 4 times as needed. YIELD: 6 - 8 servings.

SPRINGTIME SPINACH QUICHE

4 slices bacon	4 eggs, beaten lightly
2 c. shredded Swiss cheese	½ tsp. salt
1 c. chopped spinach	½ tsp. ground nutmeg
1½ tbsp. flour	9 - inch prepared pastry shell
1¼ c. cereal cream	

Place bacon on plate or bacon rack. Cover with waxed paper. MW FP until crisp (3 - 4 minutes). Drain on paper towel. Break into bite size pieces.

Mix cheese, spinach, and flour in medium sized bowl. Arrange in even layer on cooked pastry. Put cream in 2-cup measure and MW FP for 3 minutes.

Whisk eggs, salt, and nutmeg in medium size bowl. Stir in cereal cream. Pour over cheese-spinach mixture. Sprinkle reserved bacon over egg mixture.

MW FP 2½ minutes. Turn dish ¼ turn. MW FP for another 2½ minutes. MW PL5 until knife inserted in centre of filling comes out clean, 12 - 15 minutes. Let stand 5 minutes before serving. YIELD: 6 - 8 servings.

ZUCCHINI OMELETTE

2	med. zucchini (about 1 lb.)	1	tsp. salt
1	med. onion, sliced	1	tsp. mixed Italian herbs,
4	eggs		crumbled
1	c. shredded Swiss cheese	¼	tsp. seasoned pepper

Trim zucchini and cut into 1-inch chunks. Arrange in an 8-cup shallow microwave safe casserole with onion slices. Cover casserole with plastic wrap, turning one edge slightly back to vent. MW FP 5 minutes. Drain liquid from casserole.

Beat eggs until foamy in a medium size bowl with a whisk; stir in shredded cheese, salt, Italian herbs and seasoned pepper. Pour over vegetables in casserole and stir to blend.

Cover casserole with a paper towel. MW PL5 for 2 minutes; remove paper towel and stir. MW PL5 another 2 minutes. Cover casserole with plastic wrap and let stand 5 minutes before serving. YIELD: 4 servings.

HINT:

— *Rehydrate dried fruits by covering with liquid and MW FP 5 minutes. Let stand 6 minutes.*

EXTRA RECIPES

FISH

FISH FILLETS - HOW TO MICROWAVE

The microwave is an excellent tool for cooking fish. Because it is a moist cooking method, fish will not be dry, provided that you do not overcook it. With a cooking time of five to seven minutes per pound, one need spend little time in the kitchen.

POINTS TO REMEMBER WHEN MICROWAVING FISH:

Always cook fish from a fresh or defrosted state. Do not cook frozen fish because it cooks so quickly that the outside will be overcooked and the inside will be undercooked.

Ideally, fish should be defrosted under cold water or slowly at power level three in the microwave. As juices accumulate while defrosting the fish, remove them and blot the fillets. Always cover fish when defrosting and be very careful not to actually cook the fish while defrosting.

A good method by which to freeze fresh fish is to place it in containers filled with water. Milk cartons are ideal, as the fish can be laid into the cartons without folding them; the thinner the fillet, the more quickly it will defrost. Fill the cartons with water, secure shut and freeze. The water protects the fillets from freezer burn. To defrost, peel away carton and run block of ice/fish under water to dissolve ice and thaw fillets.

Fish fillets can be seasoned and wrapped in lettuce leaves when cooking for a moist and delicious final product.

Because of the irregular shape of fish fillets it is often necessary to fold and double thin portions of the fillets, or overlap and place so that thick portions are along the outside edges of the cooking container and the thin portions are toward the centre. This method of placement will ensure even cooking.

Lemon juice should be added at the end of cooking, unless called for as a sauce ingredient. Because of its high acid content, lemon juice sometimes will cause the fish to become mushy if added before cooking.

Fish should generally be covered during the cooking process.

Cooking of fish should be done at full power with a time of five to seven minutes per pound. Fish will be opaque, firm, and flake at the touch of a fork when done.

Standing time is an important step in the process when cooking fish. Don't ignore it or your fish will be overcooked. Fish should remain covered during the standing time.

SHRIMP
- HOW TO MICROWAVE

Peel and devein the shrimp.

Place shrimp in a spoke pattern with the tails pointing to the centre of the cooking vessel.

Cover with plastic wrap or lid.

Microwave shrimp at full power for three to four minutes per pound.

Let stand, covered, for two to three minutes.

Shrimp will have opaque white flesh with pink markings and the fins will be pink or red in color.

LOBSTER TAIL
- HOW TO MICROWAVE

Using kitchen shears or scissors, cut a horizontal line down the centre of the top of the shell to the fin, keeping the cut just through the shell, and not through the meat. Carefully snap open and pop the meat onto the top of the shell. By doing so, the meat will sit attractively atop the shell when served.

Place the lobster tails with the meat side up in a baking dish in a spoke pattern with the fin ends pointing to the centre of the dish.

Brush with melted butter and sprinkle with paprika.

Cover with plastic wrap or lid. Microwave at full power for three to four minutes per pound.

Let stand two minutes.

Lobster meat will be white and the shell will be red when cooked.

HINT:

— *Remove plastic wrap toward yourself so steam will escape away from you and avoid painful steam burns.*

COQUILLE ST. JACQUES

As a microwave instructor and demonstrator one meets a great number of people. One student who stands out in my mind is Frances Buxton. Always sharing a smile and a good recipe - this is one of Frances' contributions.

2	tbsp. butter or margarine	¼	c. dry white wine
¼	c. butter or margarine	2	tsp. lemon juice
¼	c. fine, dry bread crumbs	¼	c. all-purpose flour
2	tbsp. Parmesan cheese	¼	tsp. salt
1	lb. small scallops	¼	tsp. marjoram
1	c. sliced fresh mushrooms	½	c. light cream
¼	c. chopped green onion	2	tbsp. fresh snipped parsley

Place 2 tablespoons butter in a small bowl. MW FP 30 - 45 seconds or until melted. Stir in bread crumbs and Parmesan cheese. Set aside. Put ¼ cup butter in 1½ quart casserole. MW FP 30 seconds to 1 minute, or until melted. Stir in scallops, mushrooms, onion, wine and lemon juice. Cover. MW PL5 for 8 - 10 minutes, or until scallops are firm and opaque, stirring every 2 minutes.

With slotted spoon transfer mixture to bowl, reserving liquid in casserole. Cover scallop mixture to keep warm. Stir flour, salt and marjoram into reserved liquid. Blend in cream. MW FP 2 - 4 minutes, or until mixture thickens, stirring after half the time. Stir in scallop mixture. Divide coquille among four 10 oz. custard cups. Sprinkle each with some of the bread crumb mixture and some parsley. Arrange filled cups in MW 2 inches apart in a ring pattern. Insert probe into centre of one dish and set to 140, or MW PL5 for 5 - 7 minutes, until hot.

If you wish, you can substitute ½ teaspoon curry powder IN PLACE OF MARJORAM to make a curry flavored dish instead.

CRAB STUFFED FISH

1	lb. sole fillets	2	tbsp. sour cream or yogurt
2	green onions, chopped	2	tsp. lemon juice
6	oz. crab		Salt & pepper, to taste
½	red pepper, chopped	¼	c. white wine
1	tsp. mustard		

Mix all ingredients except sole and wine. Place one heaping tablespoon of the mixture over one fish fillet - roll. Place rolled fish into a 3-quart round casserole dish - any leftover mixture may be placed in centre. Add ¼ cup white wine; cover with plastic wrap. MW FP 7 - 10 minutes. Let stand 5 minutes. Garnish with slices of lemon and dill. YIELD: 3 - 4 servings.

DILLED FLOUNDER DIVAN

½ tsp. crushed dried dill weed	1 c. sliced carrots
10¾ oz. can condensed cream of celery soup	10 oz. pkg. frozen broccoli spears, thawed & cut in 1-inch lengths
1 lb. fillets of flounder cut into 1-inch pieces	2 tbsp. dry white wine
	Buttered bread crumbs

In a 2-quart round glass casserole, combine carrots and dill. Cover with glass lid. MW FP 3 - 4 minutes or until just tender.

Gently stir in soup, fish, broccoli and wine. Recover. MW FP 8 - 10 minutes or until fish flakes, stirring once.

Let stand, covered, 2 minutes. Garnish with bread crumbs and serve with rice. YIELD: 4 servings.

MICRO STYLE CREOLE

2 tbsp. flour	½ c. finely chopped green pepper
⅛ tsp. cayenne or red pepper	
2 tsp. parsley flakes	12 oz. fresh or thawed peeled shrimp
1 small onion, finely chopped	
1½ c. quick cooking rice	2 - 8 oz. cans tomato sauce
	1 small bay leaf

Combine all ingredients except bay leaf in a casserole or baking dish. Mix gently. Add bay leaf. Cover tightly with plastic wrap, venting one corner. MW FP 6 - 8 minutes, turning dish halfway through cooking time. Let stand 2 - 3 minutes. Remove bay leaf. YIELD: 4 servings.

ORANGE RUFFY IN SHRIMP SAUCE

1½ lb. orange ruffy or boneless fish fillets	¼ c. milk
	¼ c. dry white wine
3 - 4 green onions, chopped	½ c. shredded Mozzarella cheese
1 tbsp. lemon juice	
10 oz. can condensed cream of shrimp soup	2 tbsp. parsley
	4 - 5 oz. shrimp, cut in pieces
3 tbsp. flour	Toasted almonds (garnish)

Cut fish into 1-inch pieces. Combine with onion and lemon juice. Cover tightly with plastic wrap, venting one corner. MW FP 7 - 8 minutes or until fish flakes easily. Set aside, covered.

Combine soup, flour, milk and wine in a large glass measuring cup. MW FP 4 minutes, or until mixture boils, stirring twice. Add shredded Mozzarella cheese to hot soup mixture and stir until melted. Add parsley and shrimp to soup mixture and pour over fish. MW FP, uncovered 4 - 5 minutes. Sprinkle with paprika or toasted almonds.

PEPPERY FISH FILLETS WITH LIME

1	lb. cod or other whitefish fillets	⅛	tsp. coarsely ground black pepper
2	tbsp. or more lime juice	1	tbsp. chopped fresh thyme or 1 tsp. dried
⅛	tsp. cayenne pepper	3	tbsp. chopped fresh parsley
	Dash salt, optional		

In a 12 x 8 inch microwave dish, arrange fish, tucking thinner areas under, if necessary, to create even thickness.

Top with lime juice, cayenne pepper, black pepper, thyme, parsley and salt.

Cover dish with waxed paper. MW FP 6 - 10 minutes, rotating dish ½ turn if necessary, every 3 minutes. YIELD: 4 servings.

SALMON IN A CIRCLE

15	oz. can salmon	2	tbsp. chopped celery leaves
1	egg, slightly beaten	1	small onion
1	c. bread crumbs	¼	tsp. salt
½	c. cream	1	tbsp. lemon juice
¼	c. diced celery		
½	tsp. dill seed		

To get juice from lemon, MW FP 30 seconds before cutting. Cut lemon into wedges and extract juice from a wedge or two. The balance can be served with the salmon. Put drained salmon into a bowl. Remove bones and flake. Add remaining ingredients and mix thoroughly. Using a ring mold, or if you don't have one, a pie plate with a custard cup (open side up) placed in the center of it, gently press the salmon mixture into it evenly. Cover with waxed paper and MW FP 9 minutes. Let stand 5 - 10 minutes. Invert onto serving platter. Garnish with lemon wedges. Serve with sauce.

SAUCE

2	tbsp. butter	¼	c. mayonnaise
2	tbsp. flour	¼	c. chopped almonds
1	c. milk	¼	c. chopped olives

Put butter in a 2 cup measure. MW FP 45 seconds to melt. Whisk in flour to make a paste. Whisk in milk. MW FP 3 minutes, whisking every minute to avoid lumping. Remove from oven and whisk in mayonnaise. Add almonds and olives. Stir to blend. Pour over individual portions if desired.

SEAFOOD BISQUE

Taken from the Seafood Diet. You see food, you eat it!!

1 tbsp. butter	1¼ c. chicken broth
⅓ c. chopped onion	¼ c. dry sherry
¼ c. grated carrot	1 c. light cream
2 tbsp. chopped celery	6 oz. can crab meat rinsed,
¼ c. all-purpose flour	drained & flaked
¼ tsp. salt, paprika &	4½ oz. can shrimp,
dried thyme leaves	rinsed & drained
Dash pepper	

Put butter, onion, carrot and celery in a 2-quart casserole. MW FP 2 - 3 minutes, or until vegetables are tender, stirring halfway through cooking time. Stir in flour, salt, paprika, thyme and pepper. Blend in broth and sherry. MW FP 2½ - 3½ minutes or until mixture thickens, stirring after every minute. Blend in cream. Add crab meat and shrimp. MW PL5 for 8 - 10 minutes or until hot, stirring every 2 minutes.

SHRIMP STUFFED SOLE

6 tbsp. butter, divided	½ c. bread crumbs
4 ¼ oz. can shrimp	¼ c. light cream
1 tbsp. chopped parsley	1 tsp. dill weed
1 lb. sole fillets	1 tsp. paprika
2 tbsp. lemon juice	Salt to taste

Put 3 tablespoons of butter in a bowl and MW FP 45 seconds or until melted. Drain, rinse and chop shrimp and add to butter along with bread crumbs, cream and parsley. Set aside.

Put last 3 tablespoons of butter in a baking dish and MW FP 45 seconds or until melted. Cut fillets in half lengthwise and dip in melted butter. Spoon an equal amount of shrimp mixture onto each piece of fillet. Roll each piece jelly roll style and secure with a toothpick.

Stand pieces on end and place doughnut style in baking dish. Sprinkle with dill weed and paprika. Cover tightly with plastic wrap, venting at one corner. MW FP 6 - 8 minutes. Let stand 5 minutes. Fish should flake at the touch of a fork. Sprinkle with lemon juice and salt to taste.

HINT:

— **Remove tea bags from brewed tea and reheat as needed in microwave.**

SOLE ALMONDINE

¾	c. sliced almonds		Pepper to taste (white
2	tbsp. butter		pepper is nice on fish)
½	tsp. seasoned salt	1	tbsp. lemon juice
1	lb. sole fillets	1	tbsp. chopped parsley

Put almonds in a doughnut pattern in the bottom of a glass pie plate and MW FP 5 - 6 minutes, stirring every minute until golden. Set aside. Put butter in a large dish and MW FP 45 seconds or until melted. Stir in seasoned salt. Coat sole fillets with butter mixture and arrange in dish with the thickest part of the fillets to the outside. Sprinkle with lemon juice and parsley. Cover tightly with plastic wrap, venting in corner, MW FP 6 - 8 minutes, rotating dish halfway through cooking time. Let stand 5 minutes. Top with toasted almonds and serve with lemon wedges.

STUFFED TROUT OR SALMON

3 - 4 lb. trout or salmon		½	tsp. thyme
4	tbsp. butter	½	tsp. salt
1	small onion, minced	¼	tsp. rosemary
1	c. chopped celery	2	tbsp. grated Cheddar
1	tbsp. malt vinegar		cheese
⅛	tsp. pepper	3	c. soft bread crumbs

Put butter in microproof dish. MW FP 1 minute or until melted. Add onion and celery to melted butter. MW FP 3 minutes. Stir in seasonings and then the remaining ingredients. Wash and pat fish dry. Stuff. Secure stuffing opening with wooden toothpicks or sew loosely with thread. Fold tail under body to avoid over-cooking. Pierce skin in several places. Cover. MW FP 15 - 20 minutes. Let stand 10 minutes. When fish is done flesh should flake to the touch of a fork and should be opaque.

TUNA PITA POCKETS

7	oz. can tuna	3	sprinkles of pepper
	(or thereabouts)	1	c. shredded cheese
1	tbsp. chopped celery		Mozzarella, Swiss, Cheddar
1	tbsp. chopped sweet		or Combination
	pickle		Shredded lettuce
4 - 6 tbsp. salad dressing			Alfalfa sprouts
3	sprinkles salt	4	pita pocket breads

Carefully drain liquid from tuna. Put tuna in a mixing bowl and add everything except the lettuce, alfalfa sprouts and pita bread. Flake with a fork to fluff tuna and mix ingredients. Divide filling among the 4 pitas and spread filling evenly in pitas. MW each pita PL6 for 1 minute to warm filling and melt cheese. Top with lettuce and/or alfalfa sprouts.

TROPICAL SOLE

2	tbsp. butter, divided	½	c. pineapple juice
½	c. shredded carrot	1	tbsp. vinegar
2	tbsp. chopped onion	1½	tsp. brown sugar
¼	tsp. salt	1½	tsp. cornstarch
1	can crushed pineapple in its own juice	1	tsp. soya sauce
1	lb. sole fillets	¼	green pepper, julienned

Put 1 tablespoon of butter in pie plate and MW FP 45 seconds to melt. Add carrot and onion and MW FP 2 - 3 minutes until onions are softened. Drain pineapple well, reserving juice. Add ½ cup drained pineapple and salt to carrot/onion mixture. Spread an equal amount on each fillet and roll up jelly roll style and place seam side down (fasten with toothpick if necessary) in buttered pie plate. Melt second tablespoon of butter and drizzle over fish. Cover tightly with plastic wrap, venting one corner. MW FP 7 - 9 minutes. Let stand, covered, 10 minutes. While fish is standing, prepare sauce.

Combine reserved pineapple juice, vinegar, brown sugar, cornstarch and soya sauce in a measuring cup. MW FP 2 - 3 minutes, whisking every 30 seconds, until mixture boils. Stir in green pepper and remaining drained pineapple. MW FP 1 minute. Pour over fish and serve.

VEGETABLE TOPPED FISH

14	oz. fish fillets	2	chopped green onions
2	tbsp. butter	1	diced tomato
	Juice of ½ a lemon	3	tbsp. white wine
1	carrot, grated		

Place fish fillets in baking dish with thicker portions to the outside and thinner portions to the center. Sprinkle with the vegetables. Dot with butter. Sprinkle with lemon juice. Splash with wine. Cover tightly with plastic wrap, venting in corner. MW FP 5 - 6 minutes. Let stand 5 minutes. Fish should flake to the touch of a fork. Serve with Hollandaise Sauce.

HOLLANDAISE SAUCE

¼	c. butter	¼	tsp. salt
¼	c. whipping cream	1	tbsp. lemon juice
2	egg yolks		

Put butter in a 2-cup measure. MW FP 45 seconds to melt. Add balance of ingredients and whisk well. MW FP 45 seconds to 1 minute, whisking every 15 seconds. If the sauce needs further thickening, continue to MW at full power at 10 - 15 second intervals, whisking after each addition of time. Watch very carefully as overcooking will cause the sauce to curdle.

BEEF

BEEF - HOW TO MICROWAVE

Beef comes in varying levels of tenderness, depending from which part of the animal any particular cut comes. Because the cooking process is also a tenderizing process, different cuts of beef must be cooked by different methods, just as in conventional cooking.

Generally FP is used only for ground beef, beef sausages, wieners, and casseroles. Although cuts such as rib roasts, rib, wing, T-Bone, porterhouse and sirloin steaks are very tender and can be cooked in the microwave, it is my personal feeling and preference that they are best cooked conventionally. If you do use the microwave it is well suited to use in conjunction with a conventional cooking method. For example, if steaks are on sale I will buy several, barbecue them very rare, cool, wrap and freeze them and then at a later date defrost and finish them in the microwave oven.

Seventy percent power (PL7) and a moist cooking method is used on cuts such as rump, sirloin tip, and round steaks or roasts. By covering the meat and using a longer cooking time these meats adapt very well to microwave cooking.

Fifty percent power (PL5) and marinating of the meat is used on cuts such as cross rib and blade roasts. Cooking again is done with liquid and the meat cooked in a covered container.

Thirty percent power (PL3) is used on very tough cuts such as chuck roasts, short ribs & flank steak & the meat is cooked in liquid in a covered container.

These are, of course, only guidelines and exact methods are described in individual recipes.

When selecting a roast for the microwave, choose one weighing over three pounds; try to get a fairly even shape (if the roast is thick at one end and thin at the other the thin end will cook more quickly), and look for a layer of fat surrounding the outside of the roast. If there is no fat on the roast ask the butcher for some pieces which you can tie around the roast while it is cooking. The fat will impart flavor and moisture to the meat and can be removed before serving.

Foods cooked for longer than 20 minutes in the microwave will have some natural browning. Browning is the caramelization of sugars and fats, so a roast will be browned, although not exactly like it would be in a conventional oven. If you wish to enhance the natural browning, "sun tan" lotions or browning agents can be employed, such as Microbaste, Kitchen Bouquet or a homemade baster or:

(continued)

BEEF - HOW TO MICROWAVE (continued)

MICRO TANNING LOTION — FOR FOOD ONLY!

1 c. granulated sugar	1 c. water

On conventional stove top, in a heavy skillet, brown the sugar. The sweetness is removed and the sugar will get dark. Gradually and carefully add water. Heat mixture until it begins to thicken. Cool and store in a jar in the fridge. If the mixture gets too thick, thin with water or fruit juice. Add melted butter, garlic powder and spices to a portion for browning beef products. For fish add lemon juice, white wine and appropriate spices.

TO ADAPT A CONVENTIONAL RECIPE:

Use one half to one third of the conventional time, i.e. if a recipe calls for one hour of cooking in a conventional stove, cut the time to 15 - 20 minutes in the microwave oven. ALWAYS UNDERCOOK BEEF, it is always possible to add cooking time, but difficult to revive overcooked meat.

Use less liquid. Because the cooking time is short there is less time for liquids to evaporate, so reduce them by one quarter at the onset, i.e. if a recipe calls for one cup of liquid, reduce it to three quarters of a cup. If it is not possible to reduce the liquid it may be necessary to increase the thickening agent, i.e. corn-starch or flour. In stews I quite often use instant potato flakes to thicken the liquid.

Adjust seasonings. If you are using less liquids it follows that less spices will be called for.

Salt should only be added if it is added to a liquid. Do not salt the surface of the meat as salt draws out the moisture. It can be added during the standing time or just before serving.

When making stews try to cut the meat into uniform chunks. Likewise with the vegetables, the denser the vegetable, the smaller it should be cut or it can be precooked so that the components of the stew will all be ready at the same time.

Ground beef can be cooked in a microproof colander set over a bowl. This allows all the fat and excess moisture to drain away from the beef during the cooking process. When cooking meat loaf it is best to use a ring pan or a pie plate with an upright glass in the centre. This shape ensures even cooking.

Defrost beef at thirty percent power (PL3), turning over halfway through defrosting time. Always use minimum time and check meat. Beef will take four to eight minutes per pound. With ground beef, which defrosts very quickly on the surface, remove defrosted portions as they become ready. Let meat stand for five to ten minutes after defrosting to equalize the temperature before cooking.

BEEF - HOW TO MICROWAVE (continued)

Because microwaves are more readily attracted to fats and sugars you may find that fatty areas of the meat begin to get quite warm during the defrosting process and may even begin to cook. If this situation arises simply secure small pieces of aluminum foil using wooden toothpicks over the areas and only over the exact area you wish to "Shield". Shielding prevents the microwaves from penetrating the food and thus halts the cooking process.

If your microwave oven has a meat probe you can cook by temperature, in which case you should refer to the instructions in your manual. If you wish you can use a microwave thermometer in the microwave oven or you can use a conventional thermometer once the meat has been removed from the microwave. Give the thermometer at least two minutes to register.

AMERICAN STYLE MOUSSAKA

1	small eggplant, cut in half lengthwise	¼	tsp. garlic powder
		¼	tsp. pepper
½	lb. ground beef	1	tbsp. flour
¼	c. finely chopped onion	½	c. milk
1	tsp. salt	½	c. shredded Swiss cheese

Scoop pulp out of eggplant, leaving shell a half inch thick. Dice pulp. Crumble ground beef into a microproof colander. Place over casserole. MW FP 7 minutes, stirring once, until beef is no longer pink. Discard fat. To casserole add cooked beef, onion, salt, garlic, pepper and diced eggplant. Cover. MW PL7 for 15 minutes. Blend in flour and milk. MW FP until mixture thickens, about 1 minute. Blend in ¼ cup cheese. Fill eggplant shells with meat mixture. Place in 12 x 8 baking dish. Cover tightly with plastic wrap, venting one corner. MW FP 4 - 6 minutes, turning dish once during cooking. Remove plastic wrap. Sprinkle with remaining cheese. MW FP 30 seconds or until cheese melts. YIELD: 2 servings.

OVERNIGHT CASSEROLE

1	lb. ground beef	10	oz. can condensed Cheddar cheese soup
1	tbsp. minced onion		
1	c. uncooked macaroni	2	tsp. sugar
½	c. chopped green peppers	1	tsp. salt
10	oz. can tomato soup	⅛	tsp. pepper

Crumble meat in micro safe colander. Set over bowl or casserole. MW FP 3 minutes to remove excess fat. Discard fat. Combine all ingredients in 2-quart casserole. Cover. Refrigerate overnight. MW FP, covered, 20 minutes, stirring every 5 minutes. YIELD: 4 servings.

BEEF CHUNK CHILI

3   c. cooked beef, chopped
    fine
1   med. onion, chopped
1   med. green pepper,
    chopped
1   clove garlic, minced
14 oz. can kidney beans,
    rinsed & drained

19 oz. can tomatoes
5½ oz. can tomato paste
2   tbsp. brown sugar
1 - 2 tsp. chili powder
2   tbsp. vinegar
2   tsp. parsley flakes
1   tsp. salt

Combine all ingredients in a 3-quart casserole, cover, MW PL5 for 8 minutes. Stir. MW PL5 for 12 - 15 minutes. Stir once again. Let stand 10 minutes before serving. NOTE: You may want to garnish individual servings with grated Cheddar cheese. YIELD: 6 servings.

BEEF IN RED WINE SAUCE

1½ - 2 lb. sirloin steak, cut
    into 1½-inch cubes
¼   tsp. salt
2   tbsp. flour
½   c. dry red wine
½   c. water
1   c. chopped onion

1   c. sliced fresh mushrooms
    or
1   c. canned, sliced
    mushrooms, drained
1   green pepper, cut in 1-inch
    pieces

In 2-quart casserole combine steak, salt, flour, wine and water. Blend well. Cover, MW FP 9 minutes. Stir once. Stir in mushrooms, green pepper and onions. MW FP, covered, 6 minutes or until meat in tender and sauce is thickened. YIELD: 6 - 8 servings.

BURGER-STUFFED PEPPERS

6   lge. green peppers
1   lb. ground beef
1   c. quick-cooking
    rolled oats
1   small onion,
    finely chopped

1   egg, slightly beaten
8   oz. can tomato sauce
1   tbsp. Worcestershire sauce
1   tsp. salt
⅓   c. water

Scoop out peppers, set aside. Combine remaining ingredients except water, in medium bowl. Mix well. Spoon meat mixture into green peppers. Place peppers in 12 x 7 inch glass baking dish. Pour water in bottom of dish. Cover with plastic wrap. MW FP 22 minutes or until done. Let stand, covered, 5 minutes before serving. Top with catsup or chili sauce. YIELD: 6 servings.

BEEF STEW

1½ lb. boneless lean beef chuck steak, cut into ½-inch cubes	2 med. carrots, thinly sliced
	1 stalk celery, cut into ¼-inch slices
¼ c. all-purpose flour	¼ c. ketchup
2 tsp. salt	1 clove garlic, minced
¼ tsp. pepper	2 tbsp. all-purpose flour
3 med. potatoes, cut into ½-inch cubes	½ c. cold water
	10 oz. pkg. frozen green peas, thawed & drained
2½ c. hot water	

Stir beef, ¼ cup flour, the salt and pepper in 3-quart casserole until beef is coated. Add 2½ cups water, potatoes, carrots, celery, ketchup and garlic.

MW FP, covered, 5 minutes. MW PL5 until beef is tender, 40 minutes to 1 hour, stirring once or twice during cooking.

Mix 2 tablespoons flour and ½ cup cold water until smooth. Stir flour mixture and peas into stew; cover. MW PL5 until mixture thickens slightly and peas are tender, 10 to 15 minutes. Serve with rice or noodles, if desired. YIELD: 4 - 6 servings.

HINT:

— *To peel tomatoes MW each FP 1 - 1½ minutes and let stand for 10 minutes.*

BEEF STROGANOFF

1½ c. fresh sliced mushrooms	½ tsp. salt
1 med. onion, chopped	¼ tsp. pepper
1 clove garlic, minced	1 c. hot water
2 tbsp. margarine or butter	1 tbsp. sherry
1 lb. boneless beef sirloin steak, ½-inch thick, cut across grain into thin strips	1 tbsp. ketchup
	2 tsp. instant beef bouillon
	½ tsp. Worcestershire sauce
	1 c. dairy sour cream
3 tbsp. all-purpose flour	

Combine mushrooms, onion, garlic and margarine in 2-quart casserole; cover. MW FP until mushrooms and onions are tender, 2 - 4 minutes.

Shake beef, flour, salt and pepper in plastic bag until beef is coated. Stir beef and remaining ingredients except sour cream into vegetable mixture.

MW FP, covered, 5 minutes. MW PL7 until beef is tender, 20 - 30 minutes, stirring after half the cooking time. Let stand 5 - 10 minutes. Stir in sour cream until blended. YIELD: 4 - 6 servings.

HINT:

— *Melt chocolate in wrapper. Do not overcook as it will burn.*

BEEF SUPREME

This recipe comes from John. He is what you might call functionally illiterate when it comes to the kitchen. Believe it or not, this is what he cooked the day he invited his girlfriend to dinner. It must be a great recipe; it was love at first bite! John got married.

1½ lb. boneless beef chuck steak, cut into ½-inch cubes	10¾ oz. can condensed cream of mushroom soup
¼ c. all-purpose flour	10¾ oz. can condensed cream of celery soup
¾ tsp. salt	3 med. potatoes, cut into ½-inch cubes
¼ tsp. pepper	
1 med. onion, chopped	3 med. carrots, thinly sliced
2 tbsp. margarine or butter	1 tbsp. Worcestershire sauce

Shake beef, flour, salt and pepper in plastic bag until beef is coated. Set aside.

Place onion and margarine in 3-quart casserole. MW FP until onions are tender, 3 - 4 minutes.

Stir beef and remaining ingredients into onions; cover. MW FP 5 minutes. MW PL5 until beef and potatoes are tender, 45 minutes to 1 hour, stir 2 or 3 times during cooking. Let stand 5 - 10 minutes. Serve with rice, noodles or potatoes, if desired. YIELD: 6 - 8 servings.

BEEF WITH BROCCOLI

1 tbsp. oil	1 tbsp. cornstarch
1 lb. boneless steak, cut into thin strips	½ c. beef broth
1 clove garlic, finely chopped	1 tbsp. sherry
⅛ tsp. ginger	1 tbsp. soya sauce
3 - 4 c. broccoli flowerets	Toasted sesame seeds

Put oil in 12 x 8 inch dish; MW FP 2 minutes. Stir in beef, garlic, and ginger. MW FP 3½ - 4½ minutes; stir twice. Add broccoli. Cover with plastic wrap. MW FP 5 - 6 minutes or until broccoli is tender crisp; stir once.

Blend cornstarch with broth, sherry and soya sauce until smooth. Stir into beef mixture. MW FP 3 - 4 minutes or until sauce is thickened; stir once. Top with sesame seeds.

NOTE — If desired, combine beef with garlic, ginger, broth, sherry and soya sauce; marinate 30 minutes. Drain and reserve marinade to thicken. Proceed as directed above. Yield: 4 servings.

HINT:

— **Melt honey which has crystallized. BE CAREFUL, IT GETS VERY HOT.**

CHEESY BEEF STROGANOFF

3	c. cooked noodles	¼	tsp. pepper
1	med. onion, grated	7½	oz. can tomato sauce
2	tbsp. oil	½	c. sour cream
1	lb. ground beef	½	c. grated Cheddar cheese
1	tsp. salt		

Crumble ground beef into micro safe colander. Set over bowl. MW FP 3 minutes. Discard fat. Put oil and onions in 2-quart casserole. MW FP 3 minutes to saute onions. Add beef to onions.

Stir tomato sauce, sour cream and noodles into beef and onion mixture. MW FP 8 minutes. Stir, sprinkle cheese on top and MW FP another 2 - 3 minutes until cheese melts. Let stand 2 - 3 minutes. YIELD: 4 servings.

COMPANY VEAL CASSEROLE

1 -	1½ lbs. veal (chops or shoulder)		Dash basil
			Dash marjoram
1	c. sliced fresh mushrooms	10	oz. can beef gravy
1	small onion, cut in rings	1½	tbsp. flour
1	tsp. salt	½	c. sour cream
¼	tsp. pepper		Parsley
½	tsp. parsley		

Cut meat into ribbon strings. Place in 1½-quart casserole. Add mushrooms and onions. Sprinkle with seasonings. Pour gravy over (it will be thick). Cover. MW FP 5 minutes, stirring every 3 or 4 minutes.

Stir flour into sour cream. Add to gravy. Stir just to blend. Cover. Return to microwave. MW PL5, 5 minutes. Sprinkle additional parsley on top to serve. YIELD: 4 servings.

CREAMY CURRIED BEEF

2	lbs. boneless blade or round	2 -	3 tsp. curry powder
		¾	c. dry red wine
¼	c. flour	1	tbsp. Worcestershire sauce
½	c. water	½	tsp. salt
1	beef bouillon cube	1	bay leaf
2	lge. onions, sliced	1	c. sour cream or yogurt

Cut beef into thin strips. Toss meat and flour together in 3-quart casserole. Dissolve bouillon cube in ½ cup boiling water. Pour over meat. Add with all other ingredients, except sour cream, to meat mixture. Cover, MW FP 5 minutes. Stir. MW PL5, 50 - 60 minutes or until beef is fork tender, stirring 2 - 3 times during cooking. Let stand, covered, 10 minutes. Blend in sour cream or yogurt. Serve over rice or in pita pockets with sliced cucumber. YIELD: 6 - 8 servings.

GROUND BEEF STROGANOFF

1	lb. ground beef	½	tsp. paprika
½	c. chopped onion	4	oz. can mushrooms,
2	tbsp. flour		drained
1	tsp. salt	10	oz. can condensed cream
1	c. sour cream		of chicken soup

Crumble ground beef into a colander. Set over casserole or bowl. MW FP 8 minutes, stirring every 2 minutes. Discard fat. Put cooked beef into casserole. Add flour, salt, paprika and mushrooms. Thoroughly blend in soup. MW FP 6 minutes, stirring once halfway through cooking time. Add sour cream. Return to oven. MW FP 2½ minutes. Turn dish halfway through cooking time. Serve over cooked noodles or rice. YIELD: 4 servings.

ITALIAN CASSEROLE

1	lb. ground beef	6	oz. can tomato paste
½	c. chopped onion	½	c. water
½	c. chopped green pepper	½	c. milk
8	oz. cream cheese,	¼	tsp. garlic salt
	cubed & softened	¼	tsp. pepper
1	c. cooked egg noodles	¼	c. grated Parmesan cheese

Crumble ground beef into microproof colander. Set over 2-quart casserole. MW FP until beef loses pink color, 5 - 9 minutes, stirring once to break up beef. Discard fat. Put onion and green pepper in casserole; MW FP 2 minutes to soften. Add cooked, ground beef. Stir in remaining ingredients except Parmesan. MW FP 2 minutes. Sprinkle with Parmesan. MW PL7 until heated through, 5 - 7 minutes. Rotate dish quarter turn every 2 minutes. YIELD: 4 servings.

MEAT LOAF

1½	lb. lean ground beef	2	eggs, slightly beaten
1	c. soft bread crumbs	1½	tsp. salt
¼	c. toasted wheat germ	¼	tsp. pepper
½	c. milk	8	oz. can tomato sauce
1	med. onion, chopped		(optional)

In large bowl, combine all ingredients except tomato sauce until smooth. Pat mixture into 9 x 5 inch loaf dish or ring pan. Cover dish with wax paper. MW FP 15 - 16 minutes.

Let stand, covered, 5 minutes. Drain off excess juice. Invert meat loaf onto serving dish. If desired, spread heated tomato sauce over meat loaf. YIELD: 6 servings.

LASAGNE

(and you don't have to cook the noodles!)

1	lb. ground beef	2	c. creamed cottage cheese
1	tsp. seasoned salt	2	tbsp. chopped parsley
¼	tsp. garlic powder	28	oz. jar spaghetti sauce
¼	tsp. onion powder	2	c. grated Mozzarella
¼	tsp. oregano (optional)		cheese
¼	tsp. basil (optional)	½	c. grated Parmesan cheese
2	eggs	8	uncooked lasagne noodles

Put meat in colander and place over foil lined casserole. MW FP 6 minutes, stirring twice. Remove from oven and leave meat draining in colander. Remove fat from casserole and wipe clean. Put meat, spices and spaghetti sauce into casserole. Cover and MW PL6 for 6 minutes. While the sauce is cooking, in a separate bowl mix eggs with cottage cheese, parsley and ¼ cup Parmesan cheese.

In a 9 x 13 inch MW dish put 1½ cups of the meat sauce. Place a layer of uncooked noodles over the sauce. Place half of the cottage cheese mixture over the noodles and smooth evenly. Put half of the Mozzarella cheese on top of the cottage cheese. Place half of the remaining meat sauce over the cheese layer. Repeat noodles and both cheese layers ending with meat sauce. Cover tightly with plastic wrap - DO NOT VENT. MW FP 15 minutes. Rotate dish and MV PL5 for 15 minutes. Remove plastic wrap and sprinkle with remaining ¼ cup Parmesan cheese. Re-cover with plastic wrap and let stand for 20 minutes.

MY MEATBALLS

1	lb. ground beef	1	tsp. seasoned salt
1	egg	¼	tsp. garlic powder
½	c. bread crumbs	⅛	tsp. seasoned pepper
¼	c. chopped onion or	½	c. water
¼	tsp. onion powder		

Mix and shape meatballs to desired size. Place in plastic colander in a circular pattern. Place colander over a casserole which has been lined with a small piece of aluminum foil, shiny side out, to one inch in depth in the bottom of the bowl. MW FP 8 minutes, stirring once during cooking time. Cover and let stand 10 minutes while preparing sauce. Because hamburger is a ground product, adding salt will not have an adverse effect on its tenderness.

SECRET SWEET AND SOUR SAUCE

(for "My Meat Balls")

¾	c. grape jelly (the type you put on toast)	¾	c. bottled chili sauce

Combine in 2-quart casserole and MW FP 3 minutes until jelly is melted and the mixture boils. Add meatballs and MW PL5 5 - 6 minutes, covered. Let stand 5 - 10 minutes, covered. Can be thickened, if desired, with tapioca or cornstarch.

PINEAPPLE BEEF

1½ - 2 lb. flank steak, cut in slivers against the grain	Juice drained from pineapple
¾ c. soya sauce	4 tbsp. cornstarch
1½ green peppers, cut in narrow strips	1 tbsp. soya sauce
3 tbsp. salad oil	3 tbsp. vinegar
2 - 14 oz. cans pineapple tidbits, drained	6 tbsp. water
	½ c. sugar

Put steak slivers in shallow dish. Add ¾ c. soya sauce. Mix well so all the beef will marinate in the liquid. Allow to stand refrigerated at least 60 minutes. Drain.

Put green pepper strips and salad oil in a covered 2½-quart casserole dish and MW FP 3 minutes, until limp and glazed. Remove from dish. Add beef to dish in which peppers cooked. MW FP 5 minutes, stirring occasionally. Add pineapple juice (from tidbits). MW FP another 2 minutes.

Mix together flour, 1 tablespoon soya sauce, vinegar, water and sugar, blending well. Add to meat. MW FP 6 - 9 minutes or until sauce is slightly thickened. Add pineapple tidbits and peppers. MW FP an additional 2 minutes or until heated through. Serve on cooked rice. YIELD: 6 - 8 servings.

MY MEATZA PIE

1 lb. ground beef	15 mushrooms
1 small onion, finely diced	Barbecue sauce
1 egg	Green or red peppers, diced
½ c. bread crumbs	Olives, sliced
1 tsp. seasoned salt	Salami or cooked bacon
⅛ tsp. seasoned pepper	2 c. (8 oz.) grated Mozzarella cheese
Oregano to taste (optional)	
½ c. barbecue sauce	

Mix first 8 ingredients and press into a 9-inch pie plate, being sure to form a high edge or "wall". MW FP 6 minutes, covered with waxed paper. Let stand 3 minutes, covered, then put a plate over top and turn over to drain off fat and juices. Brush with extra barbecue sauce. Slice mushrooms on top. Sprinkle with crumbled cooked bacon or salami (if you chop it or dice it first, it makes it easier to cut the cooked pie), diced peppers, olives, or whatever your family likes. Lastly top with grated cheese. Do not cover. MW FP 6 minutes. Let stand 5 minutes. Cut into wedges to serve.

HINT:

— *Heat syrups for pancakes. It goes further and does not let the pancakes get cool.*

ROULADEN

6 slices bacon,
  cut into 1-inch pieces
10 oz. can sliced mushrooms,
  drained
1½ lbs. thick round steak,
  cut into 6 - 8 pieces*
¼ c. flour
2 tsp. salt

½ tsp. pepper
1 c. cold water
2 tbsp. flour
2 beef bouillon cubes,
  dissolved in
1 c. boiling water
¼ c. chopped onion

* Flatten and tenderize meat by placing between 2 sheets of waxed paper and pounding with a meat mallet.

Place bacon on a plate, cover with wax paper, and MW FP 5 - 6 minutes. Drain.

Combine mushrooms and bacon. Place an equal amount of bacon/mushroom mixture on each piece of meat. Roll up jelly-roll fashion tucking ends in. Tie with string.

Combine ¼ cup flour with salt and pepper. Dip beef rolls in flour mixture to coat all surfaces evenly. Discard excess flour. Place meat in a single layer in a 2½-quart casserole.

Combine 2 tbsp. flour and cold water, stirring until smooth. Stir in bouillon and onion and pour over meat. Cover.

MW FP 5 - 7 minutes. MW PL5 for 25 - 30 minutes, turning meat and stirring after 15 minutes. (Meat will be pinkish in the centre due to the colour of the bacon.) YIELD: 6 servings.

QUICK CABBAGE ROLLS

1 lge. head cabbage, cored
½ c. water
1½ lbs. ground beef
½ c. finely chopped onion
½ c. quick-cooking rice

1 tsp. Worcestershire sauce
½ tsp. basil
1 tsp. salt
½ tsp. pepper
8 oz. can tomato sauce

Place cabbage in 3-quart casserole dish. Pour water in bottom of dish. Cover with plastic wrap. MW FP 8 - 10 minutes until cabbage is partly cooked. Set aside.

Separate ground beef in medium mixing bowl. Stir in remaining ingredients, except tomato sauce. Remove 12 cabbage leaves from partly cooked cabbage. If veins in cabbage leaves are thick, cut thin slice off vein without cutting through leaf. Place equal amounts of meat mixture in each leaf. Roll up. Secure with toothpicks. Place in 12 x 7 inch glass baking dish. Cover with plastic wrap. MW FP 13 - 15 minutes. Pour tomato sauce over cabbage rolls. Re-cover. MW FP 2 - 3 minutes or until hot. Let stand, covered, 5 minutes before serving. YIELD: 12 large cabbage rolls.

HINT:

— *To peel peaches MW FP 15 - 20 seconds. Let stand 5 minutes.*

REUBEN LOAF

2 eggs, beaten
1 c. dark rye,
   soft bread crumbs
1 tbsp. minced, fresh parsley
1 small clove garlic, minced
12 oz. lean, cooked corned
   beef, chopped fine

1 c. canned sauerkraut,
   rinsed
¾ c. grated Swiss cheese
2 slices Swiss cheese,
   cut in half

Combine eggs, bread crumbs, parsley and minced garlic. Fold in corned beef. Put half meat mixture into 8 x 4 inch glass baking dish. Combine sauerkraut and Swiss cheese. Place on top of meat mixture. Top with remaining mixture. MW FP 4 minutes. Top cooked loaf with sliced Swiss cheese. If desired, sprinkle top with caraway seeds. MW FP another 50 seconds to melt cheese. YIELD: 4 servings.

RICE AND SPICE HAMBURGER CASSEROLE

1 lb. ground beef
1 med. onion, chopped
½ c. chopped celery
1 c. thinly sliced carrot

10 oz. can condensed golden
   mushroom soup
10 oz. can water
1 chicken bouillon cube

2 tbsp. soya sauce
¼ tsp. ground thyme

1 c. pre-cooked rice
¾ c. water

Put ground beef and onion in covered casserole. MW FP 8 minutes, stirring twice. Drain off fat. Add all ingredients, except rice and ¾ cup water. Mix well, cover. MW FP 13 minutes, stirring once. Moisten rice with ¾ cup water. Stir lightly into meat mixture. Cover. MW FP 13 Minutes, stirring once. Let stand 5 - 10 minutes. YIELD: 4 servings.

SHORT RIBS 'N BREW

3 lb. beef short ribs,
   cut into 3-inch pieces
12 oz. beer
1 med. onion, thinly sliced &
   separated into rings

2 stalks celery, thinly sliced
1 med. bay leaf
½ tsp. salt
¼ tsp. garlic salt
⅛ tsp. pepper

Place all ingredients in 5-quart casserole. MW FP, covered, 5 minutes.

MW PL5 - 25 minutes. Stir MW PL5, covered, until beef is tender, 25 - 35 minutes longer. Let stand 10 minutes. YIELD: 3 - 4 servings.

SOUPER POT ROAST

3 - 4 lb. chuck roast	2 carrots, cut into sticks
1½ oz. env. onion soup mix	2 ribs celery, cut into sticks
10½ oz. can beef broth	3 - 4 potatoes, quartered
1 onion, sliced thinly	

Place roast in 3-quart casserole that has a lid. Sprinkle dry onion soup over roast, add sliced onion, pour condensed soup over roast. Cover. MW FP 10 minutes until soup begins to boil. MW PL3 - 2 hours, adding vegetables during last 45 minutes of cooking time. You can also add garlic powder and seasoned pepper if desired. Salt after cooking.

SPICY MEXICAN CASSEROLE

1 lb. ground beef	14 oz. can tomatoes, cut in small chunks
1 green onion, chopped	
1 can mushroom soup	½ tsp. oregano
2 - 4 oz. canned green chilies, diced (depending on how hot you like your food)	⅛ tsp. garlic powder
	200 gm. bag corn or taco chips
	2 c. grated Monterey Jack, Brick or Havarti cheese
2 - 3 tsp. chili powder	

Crumble beef into a microproof colander and place over a 1½-quart casserole. MW FP 5 - 7 minutes, stirring once, until beef is no longer pink. Discard fat. Dump meat into casserole. Add onion. Blend in soup and chilies and set aside. Combine tomatoes, chili powder, oregano and garlic powder in a 4 cup measure or microproof bowl. MW FP, uncovered, 4 minutes or until boiling, stirring once during cooking. In a 7 x 12 inch dish layer one third of chips, half of meat mixture, half of tomato sauce and half of cheese. Repeat. Top with remaining chips. Cover with paper towel or waxed paper. MW FP 10 - 12 minutes. YIELD: 6 - 8 servings.

HINT:

— *To dry fresh flowers, start with fresh flowers that are still not yet fully opened. Fill a large glass dish half full with silica gel. Lay the flowers on the gel and then cover the flowers with more gel. Put a cup of water in the MW and then put in the dish of flowers. MW FP 1 - 2 minutes. Let stand overnight and then carefully remove the flowers.*

SWEET AND SOUR BEEF STEW

Jeanne makes a great straight lady; she's never quite sure when to take me seriously. When I asked her if she had a recipe and wanted to be in the book, she said, "No thanks, I think I'll wait for the movie to come out!" Then she winked and gave me this one.

1½ lb. boneless beef chuck steak, cut into ¾-inch cubes	1 med. onion, thinly sliced & separated into rings
2 tbsp. all-purpose flour	¼ c. packed brown sugar
1 tsp. salt	¼ c. vinegar
3 med. carrots, thinly sliced	¼ c. water
8 oz. can tomato sauce	1 tbsp. Worcestershire sauce

Stir beef, flour and salt in 2-quart casserole until beef is coated. Add remaining ingredients.

MW FP, covered, 5 minutes. MW PL5 until beef is tender, 50 minutes - 1 hour, stirring 2 or 3 times during cooking. Let stand 5 - 10 minutes. Serve over rice or noodles, if desired. YIELD: 6 - 8 servings.

SWISS STEAK

2 lb. boneless beef round steak	1 med. onion, thinly sliced & separated into rings
¼ c. all-purpose flour	1 med. green pepper, thinly sliced
1 tsp. salt	
¼ tsp. pepper	10¾ oz. can condensed tomato soup
1 c. thinly sliced celery	
1 tbsp. Worcestershire sauce	⅔ c. water

Trim round steak; pound well between sheets of waxed paper with a meat mallet to tenderize and flatten. Cut into 6 - 8 pieces.

Mix flour, salt and pepper. Coat beef with flour mixture. Place meat and any remaining flour mixture in rectangular baking dish, 12 x 8 inches or 10-inch square casserole.

Combine celery, onion and green pepper in small bowl. MW FP until vegetables are tender, 3 - 5 minutes. Mix with remaining ingredients. Pour over beef.

MW FP, covered, 5 minutes. MW PL5 until beef is tender, 40 - 50 minutes, rearranging pieces after half the cooking time. YIELD: 6 - 8 servings.

TANDOORI BEEF ROAST

1	c. plain yogurt	1	garlic clove, minced
1	small onion, minced	2	tbsp. tomato paste
1	tbsp. each of lemon juice & curry powder	3 -	4 lbs. beef roast, blade, cross rib or outside round
1	tsp. each of chili powder, salt & paprika	¼	c. flour Liquid gravy coloring sauce

Combine yogurt, onion, lemon juice, curry powder, chili powder, salt, paprika, garlic and tomato paste. Blend well. Pierce roast several times with a metal skewer. Place in a deep bowl and cover with marinade. Marinate, covered, in the refrigerator overnight or up to 24 hours, turning roast several times.

Drain marinade and reserve for the sauce. Brush diluted gravy browning sauce on all sides of the roast. Place roast on a microwave roasting rack or on an inverted saucer in a suitable baking dish. Cover with wax paper. Calculate total cooking time at PL5, allowing approximately 12 min./lb. for rare, 13 min./lb. for medium.

Cook half the total time. Turn roast over. Drain accumulated juices and save for the sauce. Shield outside edges along bone and fat with small pieces of foil. Re-cover with wax paper and cook remaining time. Cover loosely with foil and allow to stand 15 minutes.

Make sauce by blending flour and ½ teaspoon liquid browning agent with reserved marinade. Add cooking juices. MW FP 3 minutes. Stir. MW FP another 2 minutes. Serve sauce over thin slices of roast. Accompany roast with a tasty pilaf, a cool salad and a spicy fruit chutney. YIELD: 8 - 10 servings.

TACOS

½	lb. ground beef	2	tbsp. water
1	tsp. chili powder		Taco shells
¼	tsp. salt		Cheddar cheese, shredded
¼	tsp. garlic powder		Lettuce, shredded
⅛	tsp. pepper		Onion, finely chopped
⅛	tsp. cayenne (optional)		Tomato, chopped

Crumble beef into plastic colander. Set over bowl. MW FP 3 - 4 minutes. Pour drained, cooked ground beef into a casserole dish.

Stir in seasonings and water. MW FP 2 - 3 minutes or until meat is well done. Fill each taco shell with about 2 heaping tablespoons of meat filling. Top with remaining ingredients. YIELD: 6 tacos.

TOMATO BEEF

1	lb. flank steak	1	med. sliced onion
⅓	c. soya sauce	2	c. sliced fresh mushrooms
⅓	c. dry white wine	½	green pepper, sliced
1	tsp. sugar	1	pint cherry tomatoes
2	tbsp. cornstarch		

Cut steak across grain into thin strips. Place in 2-quart glass casserole. Combine soya sauce, wine and sugar. Pour over meat. Mix lightly to coat evenly. Allow to marinate 1 - 2 hours in refrigerator.

Stir in cornstarch, onion, mushrooms and pepper. Cover. MW FP 8 - 10 minutes, until sauce is thickened. Stir halfway through cooking time. Add tomatoes. Cover. MW FP about 1 minute or until tomatoes are heated. YIELD: 5 servings.

VEAL CUTLETS SOUTHERN STYLE

4	boneless veal cutlets, tenderized (4 oz. each)	1	tbsp. bottled brown sauce
4	oz. can mushroom stems & pieces	1	tbsp. water
		2⅜	oz. pkg. seasoned coating mix for chicken
4	slices cheese		

Place cutlets between sheets of waxed paper and pound with wooden mallet until cutlets are ¼-inch thick. Place slice of cheese on each cutlet. Divide mushrooms among cutlets. Roll meat up, beginning at narrow end, to enclose filling. Secure with toothpicks.

Combine sauce and water. Brush on meat rolls. Coat rolls with seasoned mix. Arrange rolls in a 9-inch pie plate. Cover with waxed paper. MW FP 9 - 11 minutes, giving dish ½ turn after 5 minutes. Spoon sauce which forms in bottom of dish over rolls. YIELD: 4 servings.

HINTS:

— *To make bacon bits, MW 2 strips of bacon FP 2 to 3 minutes. Let stand 3 minutes on paper towelling to drain and crisp. Crumble.*

— *Treat lemon and orange zest as herbs to save for later use.*

PORK

PORK - HOW TO MICROWAVE

Pork roasts and pork stews are particularly adaptable to the microwave oven. A danger with pork is undercooking. Because pork is not a tough meat, the cooking process is not as long as it is for beef, but because one wants to be sure that the meat is well cooked, the cooking process is slower and longer. Most pork is cooked at fifty percent power or (PL5). Standing time is also important for completing the cooking process of pork recipes.

The same principles applied to beef cookery also apply to pork in terms of size, shape, fat content and how to defrost the meat.

Cured meats differ from beef and their cooking method will be referred to in specific recipes.

A thermometer or meat probe is a valuable tool to aid in the proper cooking of pork. A microwave thermometer can be used in the oven, or a probe, if your oven is so equipped. If you are using a conventional thermometer, be sure to use it outside the microwave oven only, allowing it at least two minutes to register.

HAM STEAK WITH ORANGE GLAZE

½	c. brown sugar	2	lbs. ham steak
1	tbsp. cornstarch		cut 1 inch thick
	Dash cayenne pepper	8	whole cloves
1	tsp. orange rind	1	c. orange juice

In 10 x 6 inch baking dish, combine brown sugar, cornstarch and cayenne. Stir in orange rind and juice. Add ham steak. Turn steak in sauce two to three times to coat both sides. Push cloves into fat surrounding steak. MW FP, uncovered, 10 minutes, stirring twice. Spoon sauce over ham. MW FP, covered, another 7 minutes. Let stand, covered, 5 minutes. Stir. Serve. YIELD: 3 - 4 servings.

BARBECUE SAUCED PORK STEAKS

½	tsp. salt	1	tsp. dry mustard
⅛	tsp. pepper	1	tsp. Worcestershire sauce
1	c. ketchup	4	butt or shoulder pork
¼	c. white vinegar		steaks or 8 trimmed
2	tbsp. demerara sugar		deboned pork chops
1	tbsp. chopped onion		

Combine all ingredients except pork in a baking dish and MW FP 2 - 3 minutes or until mixture boils. Put pork in sauce and place in a single layer sauced side up. Cover with waxed paper. MW PL5 for 15 minutes. Turn steaks over and MW PL5 for 10 - 15 minutes longer. Cover dish with foil or saran or lid and let stand 10 minutes.

CHEESY BEAN POT

¼ c. chopped onion	2 tbsp. brown sugar
¼ c. chopped green pepper	1 tsp. prepared mustard
2 - 14 oz. cans pork & beans	1½ c. cubed meat (bologna, salami)
1 tbsp. instant coffee	
2 tbsp. chili sauce or ketchup	Dash seasoned pepper
2 tsp. molasses	1 c. Cheddar cheese cubes

Combine all ingredients except cheese cubes. MW FP 5 minutes, stirring frequently. Add cheese cubes. MW FP an additional 2 minutes. Serve on split, toasted buns. YIELD: 4 - 5 servings.

BARBECUE SAUCED SPARERIBS

3 lbs. spareribs, cut into serving pieces	7½ oz. can tomato sauce
1 med. onion, chopped	2 tbsp. brown sugar
1 clove garlic, minced	1 tbsp. Worcestershire sauce
¼ c. vinegar	1 tsp. salt
¾ c. chili sauce	¼ tsp. pepper

Place spareribs in glass baking dish approximately 13 x 9 inch. Cover with plastic wrap. MW FP 15 minutes, stirring and rearranging after 7 minutes. Drain off excess fat. Turn ribs over. Arrange onion and garlic on top. Combine remaining ingredients in small bowl. Pour sauce over ribs. Cover with plastic wrap. MW PL5 for 30 minutes. Stir and rearrange after each 10 minute period until tender. Allow to stand 5 minutes before serving. YIELD: 4 -6 servings.

HAWAIIAN FRANKS

10 oz. can tomato sauce	1 tbsp. prepared mustard
10 oz. can pineapple tidbits plus juice	2 tbsp. chopped onion
¼ c. brown sugar	½ tsp. chili powder
2 tsp. vinegar	1 lb. pkg. wieners, cut in bite-size pieces
½ c. water	

Combine all ingredients. MW FP 3 - 5 minutes. Thicken if desired. Serve over rice. YIELD: 4 servings.

IRISH PORK STEW

3	lbs. pork shoulder	1	tsp. salt
½	lb. side bacon		Pepper to taste
6	med. potatoes	2	c. real chicken broth,
10	small onions		if available, or
2	tbsp. finely chopped		chicken cube stock
	parsley	4	tbsp. flour
1	tsp. thyme	2	tbsp. soft butter

Trim pork and cut into ¾-inch cubes. Cut bacon into 1-inch pieces. Peel potatoes and cut into even, not too thin slices. Peel onions and cut into halves. Arrange ⅓ of the potatoes in a layer on the bottom of a 4-quart casserole. Cover with a layer of pork, then a layer of bacon and some of the onions. Seasoning between layers, repeat layers, ending with onions. Pour broth over ingredients. Cover. MW FP 20 minutes, or until liquid begins to boil.

MW PL5 for 50 minutes. Make a paste of the flour and butter. Add some of the casserole liquid and whisk. Add enough liquid until it becomes easy to pour and then return this to the casserole. MW FP 3 - 5 minutes or until the casserole is thickened.

Let stand, covered, 10 - 15 minutes. The meat, although thoroughly cooked, will have a slightly pinkish color to it; this is because it was not prebrowned.

PORK LOIN ROAST

3 - 4 lb. pork loin roast		½	c. apricot jam
String		½	c. barbecue sauce

Combine jam and barbecue sauce in a 2-cup measure and MW FP 1-2 minutes to melt. Choose an evenly shaped roast. Tie well. Put fat side up on a rack and cover with waxed paper. MW FP 10 minutes. Lift waxed paper and paint roast all over with glaze. Re-cover with waxed paper. Insert meat probe and set oven to PL5. Set temperature to 180. Brush with glaze every 15 minutes, or if you do not wish to "watch" the roast, simply wait until it is cooked and glaze before standing time. When the oven shuts off and the internal temperature is 180, glaze the roast, wrap in foil and let stand 10 to 15 minutes. Slice, reglaze and MW FP 1 - 2 minutes to warm glaze.

ALTERNATE GLAZE

14	oz. can pineapple slices	1	tbsp. cornstarch
¾	c. pineapple juice	¼	c. bottled chili sauce

While roast is wrapped and doing standing time, blend pineapple juice and cornstarch in a 2-cup measure. Stir in chili sauce. MW FP 3 - 4 minutes. Sauce must boil and it will be thickened and clear. Put pineapple slices in MW and MW FP 1 - 2 minutes to heat. Before serving roast, cut slices into it; place a pineapple slice in each pocket and then pour hot glaze over roast.

SAVORY SAUSAGE HASH

4	med. onions, coarsely chopped (about 4 cups)	4	med. potatoes, scrubbed and unpeeled, cut into large dice (try to cut in even pieces)
3	cloves garlic, peeled and minced		
1	lb. bulk hot spicy sausage	1	tsp. salt
¼	c. all-purpose flour	2	c. milk

Place onions and garlic in 3-quart microwave casserole. Cover with waxed paper. MW FP 3 - 5 minutes, until onions are transparent.

Add potatoes, re-cover with waxed paper and MW FP 14 - 18 minutes, until largest pieces are tender when pierced with fork. Set aside.

Place sausage in 1½-quart microwave measuring bowl or casserole. Cover with waxed paper and MW FP 5 - 8 minutes, breaking up with fork every 2 minutes, until no pink remains in sausage.

When cooked, crumble sausage loosely with fork, but do not drain (there should be about ¼ cup or 50 mL drippings). To un-drained sausage, add flour and salt.

Mix well, then stir in milk, MW FP 8 - 12 minutes, stirring every 3 minutes, until smooth and thickened.

Pour sausage gravy over potatoes and onions and gently stir to mix well. Just before serving, return casserole to oven to reheat. MW FP 3 - 7 minutes, if necessary. YIELD: 4 servings.

MAPLE BACON

1	lb. slab peameal or back bacon	1	clove garlic, minced
¼	c. orange juice	½	c. maple syrup
1½	tsp. vinegar	1	tsp. prepared mustard

Place bacon, fat side down on roasting rack in glass baking dish. Cover with waxed paper. MW FP 4 minutes. Drain fat. Rotate dish ¼ turn. Combine orange juice, vinegar, garlic, maple syrup and mustard. Set aside. Place bacon, fat side up on rack. Pour sauce over bacon. Cover with waxed paper. MW PL5 for 6 - 10 minutes or until microwave probe or thermometer reads 150 degrees Fahrenheit, when inserted in centre of meat. During the cooking period, baste bacon occasionally. Cover bacon and let stand before serving.

SCALLOPED HAM

Bob comes from over the Pond as they say, Great Britain, and although the only thing he could offer of his own was his willingness to taste test all the recipes, he did offer this one from his wife's collection.

3	tbsp. butter	⅛	tsp. cayenne pepper
⅓	c. chopped onion (1 small)	2½	c. milk
2	tbsp. all-purpose flour	4	c. thinly sliced unpeeled
1	tsp. salt		potatoes (5 medium)
¼	tsp. freshly ground	2	c. cubed cooked ham
	black pepper		(about ½ pound)

Place butter and onion in 2-quart microwave casserole. Cover. MW FP 3 - 5 minutes, until onion is transparent.

Stir in flour, salt, cayenne and black pepper until smooth. Stir in milk. MW FP 8 - 12 minutes, whisking every 3 minutes, until smooth and slightly thickened.

Into sauce, layer half of potatoes, all of ham, then remaining potatoes. Press potatoes into dish, spooning sauce over top. Cover, MW FP 19 - 23 minutes, stirring to mix potatoes and ham after 10 minutes. YIELD: 4 - 6 servings.

SPICY PORK AND BEAN THREADS

½	lb. lean ground pork	1	tsp. sesame oil
1	tsp. soya sauce	1	tbsp. peanut oil
½	tsp. rice wine	1	tbsp. minced green onion
½	tsp. sesame oil	1	tsp. fresh ginger root,
4	oz. bean threads		peeled & minced
2	c. chicken broth	2	tbsp. Chinese chili paste
2	tbsp. soya sauce		Green onions,
1	tsp. sugar		minced (garnish)

Combine pork, 1 teaspoon soya sauce, ½ teaspoon rice wine and ½ teaspoon sesame oil. Stir well with a fork to separate and completely coat the meat. Set aside for 20 minutes. Place bean threads in a shallow bowl. Pour in warm water to cover and let soak 5 minutes. Drain, cut into 3-inch lengths and place in a bowl. Cover with plastic wrap and set aside. Combine chicken broth, 2 tablespoons soya sauce, 1 teaspoon sugar and 1 teaspoon sesame oil. Set aside. Place the peanut oil, green onion and ginger root in a MW skillet and MW FP 4 minutes, stirring once. Add pork, stirring with a fork to completely combine all ingredients. MW FP 3 minutes, stirring halfway through, breaking up any chunks. Stir in chili paste and MW FP 1 minute. Add prepared bean threads. Stir the chicken broth mixture and add to skillet. Stir everything well. Cover with lid or waxed paper and MW FP 4 minutes. Let stand 3 - 4 minutes. Standing time will finish cooking and allow bean threads to absorb liquid. Garnish with chopped green onions. Serve with boiled rice.

PORK LOIN BRAISED IN MILK

3 lb. rib end pork roast	1 tbsp. butter
1 tbsp. vegetable oil	2½ c. milk

Heat vegetable oil and butter together in stove top proof casserole on medium high heat on conventional stove top. Brown pork in hot fat on all sides. Season with pepper and herbs. Remove from heat and add milk.

Cover casserole, but allow opening for steam to escape. MW FP 10 minutes, then MW PL5 for 1 - 1½ hours, turning the roast halfway through the cooking time. When the roast is done, wrap in foil and let stand 10 minutes while preparing sauce.

To make sauce, remove excess fat from braising liquid and stir in 1 tablespoon of warm milk to smooth out the sauce. Stir well to loosen any pork bits at the bottom of the casserole. Slice roast and serve with sauce.

SOUTHWESTERN STYLE PORK CHOPS

4 pork chops, cut ½-inch thick	1 c. finely crushed taco flavored tortilla chips
⅓ c. taco sauce	

Trim chops. Dip both sides of each chop in taco sauce and then in the crushed tortilla chips to coat well. Place on a rack in a baking dish with the thickest portion of the chops pointing to the outside of the dish. Cover with waxed paper. MW PL5 for 8 minutes. Rotate dish ¼ turn. MW PL5 for 8 - 10 minutes, or until tender. Remove chops using a spatula so as not to disturb coating.

STUFFED PORK CHOPS

½ c. milk	1⅝ oz. env. brown gravy mix
¼ c. butter	8 thin rib pork chops (about
2 c. dry seasoned bread stuffing	1½ lbs.), trimmed of fat

Combine milk and butter in medium size glass mixing bowl. MW FP 2 - 3 minutes or until butter is melted. Stir in bread stuffing and mix well. Set aside.

Sprinkle one side of 4 chops with half of the dry gravy mix. Place seasoned-side-down in 2-quart 8 x 8 inch glass baking dish. Spoon dressing on top of each chop. Place remaining chops on top of dressing. Sprinkle with remaining gravy mix. Cover with plastic wrap MW FP 12 - 15 minutes or until fork tender. Let stand, covered, 5 minutes before serving. YIELD: 4 servings.

SWEET AND PUNGENT PORK

2	tbsp. cornstarch	8	oz. jar sweet mixed pickles
2	tbsp. dry sherry	4	tbsp. light soya sauce
2	lbs. lean, boneless pork	2	tbsp. cornstarch
1	tbsp. peanut oil	2	tbsp. water
4	cloves garlic, minced	2	tomatoes,
16	oz. can pineapple chunks		cut into 16 wedges

Combine 2 tablespoons cornstarch and sherry in a large bowl and stir until completely blended. Cut pork into 1-inch cubes. Stir into sherry mixture and coat all pieces well. Set aside 20 minutes. Combine oil and garlic in a 4-cup measure and MW FP 2½ minutes, or until garlic is golden. Drain pineapple and pickle juices into garlic and add soya sauce. Cover with waxed paper and MW FP 4 minutes or until boiling. Remove garlic and discard. Add pineapple and pickles. Re-cover and MW FP 3 minutes. Set aside. Place pork with marinade in a single layer in a microwave skillet. Cover. MW FP 7 - 9 minutes, stirring twice during cooking. Combine 2 tbsp. cornstarch with water and stir into reserved sauce until completely blended. Cover with waxed paper and MW FP 2½ minutes, stirring once during cooking, until sauce is clear and thickened. Pour over pork, add tomato wedges and re-cover. MW FP 2 minutes, or until heated through, or brown pork in marinade on stove top. Mix into sauce and MW FP 12 - 15 minutes, stirring once during cooking.

SWEET AND SOUR PORK
(ONE OF MY FAVORITES)

3	lbs. pork shoulder	1½	tsp. Worcestershire sauce
4	tbsp. flour	⅓	c. sugar
2	tsp. powdered ginger	1½	tsp. salt
	Vegetable oil	½	tsp. pepper
¼	c. flour	1	red pepper, julienned
10	oz. can pineapple chunks	8	oz. water chestnuts
	& juice	2	tbsp. bottled chili sauce or
¼	c. white vinegar		bottled barbecue sauce
¼	c. light soya sauce		

Trim pork and cut into ¾-inch cubes. Put 4 tablespoons flour and ginger in a plastic bag and shake to mix. Add a handful of pork cubes and shake to coat. Remove and add more pork and repeat until all pork cubes are coated. Using a 3-quart stove top proof glass casserole, brown cubes in a couple of tablespoons of vegetable oil on conventional stove top. In a 4-cup measure combine flour with pineapple juice and add enough water to get 1½ cups liquid. Add vinegar, soya sauce, Worcestershire sauce, sugar, salt and pepper. MW FP 7 minutes, stirring once or twice. Add to meat. Cover casserole with lid or plastic wrap and MW PL5 for 45 minutes. Check to be sure there is enough liquid, if it is too dry add a bit more pineapple juice if you have some or add a bit of water. Re-cover and continue to cook for another 15 minutes at PL5. Add red pepper, pineapple, sliced water chestnuts and chili sauce. MW FP 10 minutes. Let stand, covered, 10 - 15 minutes. Serve with rice.

WURST MIT KRAUT

6	tbsp. butter or margarine	½	c. beef broth
1½	c. chopped onion	¼	tsp. caraway seeds
2	c. sliced apples	¼	tsp. pepper
2 -	16 oz. cans sauerkraut, drained & rinsed	6	Knackwurst sausages, (approx. 3 oz. each)

In 12 x 8 inch dish, combine butter and onion. MW FP 3 - 3½ minutes. Stir in apples. MW FP 3 - 4½ minutes. Stir in sauerkraut, broth, caraway and pepper.

Score Knackwurst diagonally and arrange on sauerkraut mixture. MW FP 8 - 9 minutes. Rearrange Knackwurst once. Let stand, covered, 5 minutes. YIELD: 6 servings.

HINT:
— *Plump dried fruits for fruit cakes in brandy or rum.*

POULTRY

CHICKEN - HOW TO MICROWAVE

Chicken can be easily and quickly cooked in the microwave oven. Although some recipes do not adapt easily, i.e. fried chicken, a number of tasty and easy to prepare dishes can be made. If desired the microwave oven can be used in conjunction with conventional cooking methods to shorten cooking time. For example, three pounds of chicken parts cooked at FP for 10 - 15 minutes and then barbecued will result in a moist and delicious finished product. The microwaving process seems to melt off some of the fat under the skin, thus avoiding flare ups on the barbecue. There will be no raw meat around the bones as is often experienced when trying to barbecue raw chicken. Further, the barbecuing time will be reduced.

To microwave chicken pieces I personally prefer to remove the skin, although this is not necessary and is not necessarily stated in recipes. It is a personal choice only. Chicken cooks best when raised off the bottom of the pan in which it is cooking. Not raising the meat will result in a somewhat "stewed" or "steamed" product. This, of course, only applies to pieces being cooked in a coating or crumb topping. If the recipe calls for the chicken to be cooked in a sauce, then of course there is no need to raise it.

Whole, roasted chickens cook quickly and are very moist. Rinse bird and pat dry. Put an onion and seasoning inside the cavity. Tie legs and wings loosely with string. Place breast side down on a rack or inverted saucers in a baking dish. MW FP for 9 minutes per pound for fryer type chickens or MW PL7 for roasting chickens. After half of the estimated cooking time drain off excess drippings (reserve for gravy if desired) and using a pair of clean rubber gloves turn the bird breast side up for the last half of the cooking time. If there are any brown spots or if wing tips or drum sticks are overcooking, simply shield with bits of aluminum foil, shielding only the spots you wish to cease cooking. When time is done, cover with aluminum foil tent and allow to stand for 10 - 15 minutes. Internal temperature of the bird should be 180 - 185 degrees Fahrenheit and legs should move freely at the joint. Juice should run clear, not pink. Always cook chicken from a fresh or defrosted state.

CHICK 'N SWISS CASSEROLE

2	tbsp. flour	½	c. chopped green pepper
½	tsp. salt	¼	c. dry white wine
3	c. cubed cooked chicken	1 -	10¾ oz. can cream
1	c. grated Swiss cheese		mushroom soup
1	small onion, sliced		

Combine all ingredients in casserole. Stir gently to mix. Cover tightly with plastic wrap, venting one corner. MW FP 9 - 11 minutes stirring once during cooking. Let stand 5 minutes. YIELD: 6 servings.

CORNISH HEN A L'ORANGE

¼ c. butter or margarine	1 tsp. salt
1 tsp. paprika	1 lge. onion, quartered
1 tsp. browning agent	Orange sauce
4 - 12 oz. Cornish Game Hens	(recipe follows)

Place butter or margarine, paprika and browning agent in 2-cup glass measure. MW FP 1½ minutes or until melted. Stir. Salt cavities of hens. Fill each cavity with ¼ onion. Tie legs and wings to body. Place hens in 2-quart glass baking dish, breast side up. Brush with seasoned melted butter or margarine. Point drumsticks toward centre. MW FP 30 - 35 minutes or until microwave oven thermometer registers 170° F. Let stand 5 minutes. Pour Orange Sauce over hens. Serve immediately. YIELD: 4 servings.

ORANGE SAUCE

2 tbsp. butter or margarine	1 - 2 tbsp. Grand Marnier or other orange-flavoured liqueur, if desired
1½ tbsp. cornstarch	
¼ c. sugar	
¼ c. brown sugar, packed firmly	½ c. frozen orange juice concentrate

1 c. water	2 tbsp. orange peel, grated

Combine all ingredients, except liqueur in 4-cup glass measure. Mix well. MW FP 3 minutes. Stir. Continue cooking in microwave oven 2 minutes or until boiling. Stir in Grand Marnier or other liqueur if desired. YIELD: 1½ cups.

CORNISH HEN WITH STUFFING

2 Rock Cornish Game Hens	1 tsp. grated orange peel
Sherry	1½ c. dry bread cubes
2 tbsp. margarine	2 tbsp. orange juice
¼ c. chopped onion	Paprika
2 tbsp. chopped celery	1 tbsp. orange marmalade
2 tbsp. chopped walnuts	1 tsp. bottled steak sauce

Rub inside of hens with sherry. Put margarine, onion and celery in casserole. MW FP 2 minutes. Add nuts, peel and bread. Stir to combine. Add orange juice and mix well. Stuff hens. Sprinkle with paprika. Place breast side up on a rack or inverted saucer. MW PL7 for 10 minutes. Combine marmalade and steak sauce and brush on hens. MW FP 1 minute. Cover with foil tent and let stand 5 minutes. Hens are cooked when leg joint moves freely and juices run clear, not pink.

CORNISH HEN WITH APRICOT GLAZE

2 -	1½ lb. Cornish Hens	1	tsp. Worcestershire sauce
⅓	c. apricot preserves	¼	tsp. nutmeg
1	tbsp. honey	¼	tsp. browning agent
1	tbsp. butter or margarine		(optional)
2	tsp. lemon juice		Dash pepper

In a 2-cup measure combine everything except hens. MW FP 1 - 1½ minutes, or until butter melts. Stir. Set aside.

Defrost hens if frozen. Remove and discard giblets. Rinse hens and pat dry. Split each hen lengthwise through breastbone and backbone into two halves. Arrange halves skin side down in 8 inch square baking dish. MW FP 10 minutes. Turn pieces over. Brush with glaze. MW FP 8 - 11 minutes longer, or until juices run clear. Reheat remaining glaze and serve with hens. YIELD: 2 servings.

CHICKEN AND JULIENNE VEGETABLES

4	boneless chicken breasts or thighs	1	zucchini
2	lemons	½	tsp. salt
1	potato	¼	tsp. pepper
3	carrots	¼	tsp. ground ginger

Place chicken breasts in a single layer in casserole, top with lemon, vegetables and seasonings as above. Cover with plastic wrap, leaving one corner open to vent. MW FP 10 minutes; let stand covered. YIELD: 4 servings.

CHICKEN DIVAN CASSEROLE

2 -	10 oz. pkg. frozen broccoli spears	1	tsp. lemon juice
4	half chicken breasts, skinned & boned	½	tsp. mustard powder
		1	c. sliced fresh mushrooms
2 -	10¾ oz. cans cream mushroom soup	¾	c. grated sharp Cheddar cheese
½	c. mayonnaise	½	c. seasoned croutons

MW broccoli in pkgs. at FP 3 minutes to partially defrost. Place chicken in an 8 x 12 inch oblong baking dish. Cover with plastic wrap. MW FP 4 - 5 minutes or until barely done. Stand 1 minute. Remove chicken and slice. Arrange broccoli spears in the baking dish. Place sliced chicken over the broccoli. Combine soup, mayonnaise, lemon juice and mustard. Pour over chicken. Sprinkle with mushrooms, cheese and croutons. Cover with plastic wrap. MW FP 6 minutes. For a brown, crisp topping, place under the broiler for 4 minutes. YIELD: 4 - 5 servings.

CHICKEN MARENGO

2½ - 3 lb. broiler-fryer chicken, cut up
8 oz. fresh mushrooms, sliced
1½ oz. pkg. spaghetti sauce mix
16 oz. can whole tomatoes
¼ c. white wine

In 12 x 8 inch baking dish arrange chicken pieces, skin side up, with meatiest portions toward outside of dish. Cover with waxed paper. MW FP 10 minutes. Drain.

Turn pieces over; top with sliced mushrooms. Combine spaghetti sauce mix, tomatoes and wine, stirring to break up tomatoes. Pour over chicken. Cover. MW PL7 for 20 - 23 minutes, or until chicken near bone is no longer pink, turning pieces over after half the time. Let stand, covered, for 5 minutes. YIELD: 4 - 6 servings.

CHICKEN ROULADEN

Tickling the typewriter — Ollie and the fastest fingers in the West spend many a day at the keyboard typing recipes. Ollie is one of the freelance typists who types recipes for cook books day after day. When Ollie comes across a recipe and tells you it's a special one, you have to believe her, because Ollie has seen 'em all. Here's one that tickled not only the typewriter, but also Ollie's fancy!

1 c. chopped mushrooms
¼ c. chopped onions
¼ c. chopped celery
1 small garlic clove, minced
1 tbsp. olive oil or butter
2 tbsp. seasoned bread crumbs
¼ tsp. salt
Dash pepper
2 whole boneless chicken breasts, skin removed
¼ c. seasoned bread crumbs
½ tsp. dried parsley flakes
Mushroom sauce, (page 65)

In 1-quart casserole combine mushrooms, onion, celery, garlic and oil. MW FP 2 - 4 minutes, or until tender. Stir in 2 tablespoons bread crumbs, salt and pepper.

Place chicken breasts between waxed paper. Pound with meat mallet to flatten to ¼ inch thickness. Spread half of stuffing mixture in center of each. Fold sides of chicken over stuffing; secure with wooden pick. Mix ¼ cup bread crumbs and the parsley flakes. Roll chicken in mixture to coat.

Place in 8 x 8 inch baking dish. Cover with waxed paper. MW FP 7 - 10 minutes or until chicken is no longer pink, rearranging once during cooking. Serve with mushroom sauce.

Prepared, stuffed breasts can be frozen at this point. Wrap tightly in plastic and freeze up to one month. To cook, unwrap, place frozen pieces in baking dish and cover with waxed paper. MW PL3 for 5 minutes, then MW FP 10 - 12 minutes, rearranging once, until chicken is no longer pink.

MUSHROOM SAUCE

2 c. sliced mushrooms	1 tbsp. plus 1½ tsp. all-purpose flour
¼ c. chopped onion	
1 tbsp. plus 1½ tsp. butter or margarine	⅛ tsp. pepper
	½ c. whipping cream
¼ tsp. salt	¼ c. white wine

In 1-quart casserole combine mushrooms, onion and butter. MW FP 2 - 3 minutes, or until tender. Stir in flour, salt and pepper. Blend in cream. MW FP 2 - 3½ minutes or until thickened and bubbly, stirring once or twice. Mix in wine. MW FP 30 seconds, or until heated. YIELD: 1½ cups.

CHICKEN WITH MUSHROOM SAUCE

2½ - 3 lb. broiler-fryer chicken, cut up	8 oz. fresh mushrooms, sliced
10¾ oz. can condensed golden mushroom soup	½ tsp. seasoned salt
	⅛ tsp. pepper
¼ c. sherry	

Arrange chicken pieces in 12 x 8 inch baking dish, skin side up, with meatiest portions toward outside of dish. Cover with waxed paper. MW FP 10 minutes. Turn pieces over. Drain.

Mix soup, sherry, mushrooms, salt and pepper; pour over chicken.

Cover. MW PL7 for 20 - 23 minutes, or until chicken near bone is no longer pink, turning pieces over after half the time. Let stand, covered, for 5 minutes. YIELD: 4 - 6 servings.

COQ AU VIN

1 c. all-purpose flour	8 oz. fresh mushrooms, sliced
2 tsp. salt	
¼ tsp. pepper	1 garlic clove, finely chopped
3 lb. frying chicken, cut in serving pieces	1 bay leaf
	1 tbsp. snipped parsley
1 c. red wine	3 slices bacon, cut in 1-inch pieces
2 tbsp. brandy	
1 lge. onion, quartered	

Combine flour, salt and pepper in a plastic bag. Drop in each piece of chicken, one at a time and shake until coated. Set aside. Place bacon pieces in a 2-quart casserole. MW FP until almost crisp. Whisk remaining seasoned flour into bacon/dripping mixture. Whisk in wine and brandy. Gently stir in onion, mushrooms, garlic, parsley and bay leaf. Place chicken into mixture in casserole. Cover tightly. MW FP 15 minutes. Remove cover. Stir. Do not re-cover. MW FP 10 minutes or until chicken is fork tender. Cover and let stand 5 - 10 minutes. Be sure to remove bay leaf before serving. YIELD: 4 - 6 servings.

HONEY GARLIC CHICKEN OR CHICKEN WINGS

1 c. honey	Juice of 1 orange
¼ c. soya sauce	3 lb. frying chicken,
2 tbsp. cornstarch	cut in pieces or
2 tbsp. water	30 wings, disjointed
4 - 5 garlic cloves, mashed	(discard tips)
Zest of 1 orange	

Mix marinade ingredients in a 2-cup measure and MW FP until melted. Stir well. Put chicken pieces into casserole or empty ice cream pail and pour marinade over. Marinate 24 - 48 hours.

Arrange chicken pieces in a 12 x 8 inch baking dish with thickest portions toward outside of dish, skin side up. Cover with waxed paper. MW FP 10 minutes. Drain. Turn pieces over.

Pour marinade over chicken. Cover. MW PL7 for 9 minutes, turn chicken pieces over. MW PL7 for 9 - 11 minutes or until chicken near bone is no longer pink. Remove to serving platter. Cover and let stand.

Blend cornstarch with cold water. Stir into hot cooking liquid. MW FP 2 - 3 minutes or until thickened. Stir. Serve with chicken.

If using wings place in a spoke pattern on serving platter. MW FP 9 minutes per/pound.

FRUITED, PECAN STUFFED CHICKEN BREASTS

4 whole chicken breasts, boned & skinned	1 tbsp. flour
1 med. banana, mashed	1⅓ c. cubed day old bread, packed
¼ c. frozen orange juice concentrate, thawed	⅓ c. chopped pecans
¼ c. dark corn syrup	3 tbsp. butter or melted margarine
1 tbsp. lemon juice	

Combine bread, pecans and butter. Wash and pat chicken dry. Spoon equal portions of bread mixture on each breast. Fold and secure with toothpicks.

Place seam side down in a round casserole or baking dish or in a square dish placing in a circular pattern with thickest portion facing to outside of dish.

Combine banana, orange juice, corn syrup and lemon juice. Spoon over chicken. Cover tightly with plastic wrap, venting in one corner.

MW FP 15 - 17 minutes, turning dish every five minutes. Let stand 5 minutes.

To serve, cut each breast in half. YIELD: 8 servings.

PARMESAN CHICKEN

4	deboned chicken breasts	⅛	tsp. garlic powder
1	egg	¼	c. margarine or
1	tbsp. water		vegetable oil
½	c. flour	1	garlic clove, chopped
¼	tsp. salt	2	tbsp. lemon juice
	Dash pepper	1	c. grated Mozzarella cheese

Whisk egg with water. Combine flour with salt, pepper and garlic powder. Combine bread crumbs with Parmesan cheese. Dip chicken breasts in egg wash, flour mixture, egg wash then bread crumb mixture. Fry in margarine and chopped garlic, on conventional stove top until golden. Place chicken in microproof dish and sprinkle with lemon juice. Cover with waxed paper. MW FP 3 minutes. Sprinkle with Mozzarella cheese. MW FP 30 seconds to melt cheese. YIELD: 4 servings.

PEACH GLAZED CHICKEN

4	chicken pieces (about 1½ lbs.)	1	tbsp. Dijon mustard
		1	tsp. Worcestershire sauce
½	c. peach jam or preserves	¼	tsp. black pepper
¼	c. chili sauce or ketchup	¼	tsp. salt
2	tbsp. soya sauce	1	garlic clove, crushed

Arrange chicken pieces in a glass or microwave baking dish, so that the meatier portions are towards the outside edge of the dish. Combine remaining ingredients in a 2-cup glass measure.

MW FP 2 - 3 minutes or until mixture boils. Boil 1 - 2 minutes. Baste chicken with glaze and MW FP 10 - 12 minutes, rearranging pieces part way through cooking. Allow to rest 5 minutes before serving. YIELD: 4 servings.

POULTRY STUFFING FROM A MIX

8	oz. fresh mushrooms, sliced	8	oz. pkg. seasoned stuffing mix (about 4 cups)
½	c. chopped onion	1	c. hot water
½	c. chopped celery	2	tsp. instant chicken bouillon
½	c. margarine or butter		
1	egg	1	tsp. ground sage

Combine mushrooms, onion, celery and margarine in 1½-quart casserole. MW FP until vegetables are tender, 5 - 8 minutes.

Stir in remaining ingredients. MW FP until heated through, 4 - 7 minutes, stirring once during cooking. YIELD: 4 - 6 servings.

POULTRY STUFFING FROM SCRATCH

1	lge. onion, finely diced	½	tsp. sage
3	ribs celery, diced	½	tsp. salt
¼	c. butter, finely diced	¼	tsp. each of: pepper,
16	oz. loaf bread		garlic powder, onion
1	c. quick oats		powder, & celery salt
2	eggs		Water as needed

Put butter in large casserole and MW FP 1 minute or until melted. Add diced onion and celery and MW FP 6 minutes, stirring every 2 minutes. In a large bowl, tear bread into chunks, mix in oats, eggs and spices. Add water and mix with hands until the mixture is well moistened. If you like a moist dressing it should be the texture of drop cookie dough, if you like a dryer stuffing it should be the texture of a pie crust mixture. Add this mixture to the sauteed onion/celery and mix well. Cover and MW FP 4 - 6 minutes. Let stand 5 minutes.

The seasonings are only suggested guidelines. Start with those amounts and then add more to suit your own taste.

SAUCY CHICKEN PIECES

3	lbs. chicken pieces	1	env. dry onion soup mix
½	c. water	½	c. demerara sugar
½	c. ketchup		

Mix together everything except the chicken in a 9 x 13 inch baking dish. MW FP 3 minutes or until mixture comes to a boil. Stir to mix well. Wash chicken and remove all visible fat. Remove skin if desired. Roll chicken pieces in sauce to coat well. Arrange with thickest part to outside of dish. Cover with waxed paper and MW FP 5 minutes. Turn chicken pieces over, re-cover and MW FP 6 - 7 minutes. Let stand, covered, 5 - 10 minutes.

SEASONED CRUMB CHICKEN

¼	c. butter or margarine	1	tbsp. dried parsley flakes
16	crushed rich round crackers	½	tsp. garlic powder
			Dash pepper
½	c. grated Parmesan cheese	2 - 3	lbs. chicken pieces

Place butter in a 2-quart glass baking dish. MW FP 1 minute or until melted. Combine remaining ingredients, except chicken, in flat dish. Roll chicken in melted butter, then in seasoned crumbs. Place chicken pieces, skin side up and thick edges toward outside, in buttered baking dish. Sprinkle with remaining seasoned crumbs. Leave crumb coated poultry uncovered to crisp it. MW FP 19 - 21 minutes until meat cut near bone is no longer pink. Let stand for 5 minutes before serving. YIELD: 4 - 6 servings.

STUFFED CHICKEN BREASTS

This is one of my husband's favorite dishes, partly because it tastes so good and partly because it cooks so quickly I'm free from the kitchen . . . Kiss me honey, is what I've been saying; I've got more time since I started microwaving!

2	chicken breasts, skinned & boned	½	tsp. salt
		⅛	tsp. pepper
2	slices smoked ham	1	c. bread crumbs
2	slices Mozzarella cheese	2	eggs, beaten
4	tbsp. clarified butter	¼	c. sour cream
4	tbsp. flour		Juice of half a lemon

Place one chicken breast between two sheets of waxed paper and pound with mallet, being careful not to tear meat, until ¼-inch thick. The chicken will now be a very large flat portion.

Cut in half. Place a slice of ham on top of each piece of chicken and place a slice of cheese over the ham. Roll up jelly roll fashion, tucking in sides and keeping as tight as possible. Dip roll in beaten egg. Mix the flour with the salt and pepper. Dredge the roll in the seasoned flour. Re-dip in the egg and then dredge in the bread crumbs.

Preheat browning skillet in MW FP 4½ minutes. Add 1 tablespoon of clarified butter and tilt to coat bottom of skillet.

Add chicken rolls and MW FP 2 minutes. Turn chicken rolls over with tongs (to avoid piercing so that cheese will not leak out) and MW FP 2 - 4 minutes. Let stand while preparing sauce.

To make sauce combine sour cream, remaining beaten egg and lemon juice in a 2-cup measure. MW FP 1 - 1½ minutes, whisking every 15 seconds until sauce is thickened and fluffy. Add the rest of the clarified butter to the sauce and whisk. Let stand 30 seconds. Pour sauce over top of chicken rolls.

TERIYAKI CHICKEN WINGS

1	c. light soya sauce	2	garlic cloves, minced
½	c. sherry	1	tsp. grated fresh ginger root
½	c. sugar		
1	onion, finely chopped	1	lb. chicken wings

Mix all ingredients together except wings. Wash wings and cut into three pieces, cutting at joints. Save tips for soup. Marinate pieces in sauce for 3 hours. Place in circular pattern on a serving platter and cover with waxed paper. MW FP 6 minutes. Let stand covered 5 - 10 minutes. This marinade can be reused if brought to the boil and allowed to cook for 1 minute. Cool and store in a tightly sealed jar in the fridge. It will keep for a long time.

SWEET MUSTARD CHICKEN

¼ c. mayonnaise
¼ c. Parmesan cheese
2 tbsp. prepared mustard
⅔ c. corn flake crumbs

Skin chicken. Mix mayonnaise, cheese and mustard. Measure out ⅓ cup of the mixture and set aside in fridge. Brush chicken on both sides with remaining mixture. Coat with corn flake crumbs. MW FP 7 - 9 minutes per/pound.

TURKEY - HOW TO MICROWAVE

As with chicken, turkey should be cooked from a fresh or de-frosted state only.

I prefer to cook my stuffing separately in a casserole dish, so I put a quartered onion and few stalks of celery, and some spices in the cavity of the turkey.

Choose an evenly shaped turkey if possible. A turkey weighing 10 - 14 pounds is best suited for microwave cooking. Tie legs and wings with string, which can be cut near the end of the cooking time to allow even cooking of the thigh meat.

I baste my bird with a combination of vegetable oil, paprika, seasoned salt, garlic powder, onion powder and a bit of brandy. However, you may choose your favorite basting material and a "tanning lotion". Baste the turkey.

Place the bird breast side down on inverted saucers or a roasting rack in a baking dish.

Baste the bird as it cooks, and remove drippings from the pan as they collect as they absorb energy and lengthen the cooking time.

Turkey should be cooked at PL7 for about 9 minutes per/pound. Estimate the total cooking time of your bird and divide the time in four. Start the turkey cooking breast side down and turn over three times during the cooking time at regular intervals, using clean rubber gloves.

If wings or drumsticks begin to overcook, simply shield with aluminum foil which can be secured with toothpicks if necessary. You may wish to cover the turkey loosely with waxed paper to avoid oven splatters. When done, remove to serving platter. If your microwave oven is equipped with a probe, check for an internal temperature of 170° F. If you do not have a probe, remove turkey from oven, wrap in foil and insert a thermometer. It should reach an internal temperature of 170° F. The wrapped turkey should be left, wrapped, to stand for 20 - 25 minutes until it reaches 180° F. The drumstick bone should move freely when done and juices should run clear, not pink, when the bird is cooked.

To free up the microwave oven for other uses during the last 45 minutes of cooking time, microwave the turkey PL7 for 4 - 6 minutes per/pound and finish in the conventional oven at 350° F. for 45 minutes. You should still start the turkey breast side down and turn over as instructed. This method will also result in crispier skin.

TURKEY IN SPANISH SAUCE

¼ c. butter	2 med. hard cooked eggs,
4 cooked turkey slices	chopped
(½-inch thick)	2 tbsp. chopped gherkins or
1 lge. onion, chopped	sweet pickles
12 Spanish stuffed olives,	1 lge. tomato, quartered
chopped	

Place butter in 9 x 13 inch glass baking dish. MW FP to melt. Add turkey slices in single layer, coating with butter. Combine chopped onion, olives, eggs and pickles. Place equal amounts over turkey slices. Garnish with tomato wedges. Cover with plastic wrap. Fold back one corner to vent. MW FP 3 - 4 minutes or until heated through. YIELD: 4 servings.

TURKEY NOODLE BAKE

1 c. chow mein noodles	1 c. chopped celery
10 oz. can condensed cream	½ c. coarsely chopped
chicken soup	cashew nuts (optional)
¼ c. water	1 tbsp. instant minced onion
2 c. cooked turkey	1 tbsp. chopped pimento or
or chicken,	green pepper
cut in 1-inch cubes	1 c. chow mein noodles

In 1½-quart casserole, combine all ingredients except 1 cup chow mein noodles. MW FP, uncovered, 4 minutes or until heated through, stirring once. Sprinkle with remaining noodles. Serve immediately. YIELD: 3 - 4 servings.

HINT: (Making the most of your Microwave)
— Freshen stale or soggy cookies. Defrost cookies.

VEGETABLE STEW

2	c. cooked, cubed turkey	3	tbsp. flour
1	small onion, diced	¼	tsp. salt
1	lb. rutabaga		Dash pepper
2	med. carrots	1	tbsp. chopped fresh parsley
2	med. parsnips	1	regular-size microwavable
2	c. chicken broth		cooking bag
¼	c. white wine		

Combine turkey and onion in cooking bag.

Peel rutabaga and cut into cubes. Peel carrots and parsnips and slice.

Add rutabaga, carrots and parsnips to cooking bag along with broth, wine, flour, salt and pepper.

Tie bag loosely with string and make sure ingredients are well mixed. Place bag in 8 x 12 inch glass baking dish.

MW FP 15 minutes and stir. MW PL5 30 - 35 minutes, turning bag twice during that time, or until vegetables are tender. Stir in parsley and serve. YIELD: 4 servings.

DESSERTS

CAKES - HOW TO MICROWAVE

To bake a cake from a mix reduce liquid by 25 per cent, i.e. if instructions call for one cup water, use only ¾ cup. Mix as directed.

Prepare pan as per manufacturer's instructions. Some recommend greasing only; greasing and flouring; not greasing at all. If you want to be sure the cake will release, line pan bottom with a waxed paper or parchment paper circle.

If you do not have microwave pans (they are deeper than conventional pans) be sure to fill pans only half full or they will overflow. (Use extra batter for cupcakes).

Cakes bake best in a round or tube pan. You can create this shape by shielding corners of a square pan.

Raise pan on rack, inverted saucer or bowl - this helps the cake bake more evenly. Cover with waxed paper.

Cook one layer at a time. MW PL7 for 5 minutes. Rotate dish after half the time. MW FP 2 - 3 minutes or until centre springs back to the touch. Sides will pull away from the pan and top will still be glossy when the cake is done. Let stand on solid surface for 5 minutes. Invert onto serving plate.

HINT:
— Melt marshmallows into hot chocolate with microwave.

BANANA NUT COFFEE CAKE

When asked for a contribution for this cook book, Anna Q. Banana said "Well, I have to comb my hair first." Well, this must give you an idea of her priorities! So when Ms. Banana takes the time from her busy schedule to cook, you can be sure it will be something worthwhile! Here's a tribute to her namesake.

¼	c. oil	1	c. flour
¼	c. milk	½	c. chopped nuts
1	egg	¾	tsp. baking powder
½	c. mashed ripe banana	¼	tsp. salt
½	c. packed brown sugar	¼	tsp. baking soda

TOPPING:

¼	c. packed brown sugar	⅛	tsp. cinnamon
¼	c. chopped nuts	1	tbsp. butter or margarine, softened
1	tbsp. flour		

In medium bowl, combine oil, milk, egg, banana and sugar; add flour, nuts, baking powder, salt and baking soda. Stir only until flour is moistened.

Combine brown sugar, nuts, flour and cinnamon. Blend in butter. Set aside. Pour into greased 8 or 9 inch round dish. Sprinkle with nut topping.

MW PL 5 for 8 - 9 minutes, or until toothpick inserted near centre comes out clean. Let stand, uncovered, 10 minutes. YIELD: 8 servings.

BLACK FOREST CAKE

1¾ c. canned, pitted dark
    sweet cherries, well
    drained, divided
    (reserve 4 tbsp. juice)
¾ c. flour
⅔ c. sugar
½ tsp. baking soda
½ tsp. salt

½ tsp. vanilla
1 oz. unsweetened
    chocolate, melted
⅓ c. shortening
⅓ c. milk
2 eggs
1 oz. semi-sweet chocolate

WHIPPED CREAM MIXTURE:
2 c. (1 pint) chilled
    whipping cream

4 tbsp. reserved cherry juice

Line bottom of 9-inch round cake dish with circle of waxed paper. Place all cake ingredients except cherries and 1 egg in bowl. Blend at low speed, then beat at medium speed 1 minute, scraping bowl, constantly. Add remaining egg. Beat at high speed 1 minute, scraping bowl occasionally. Chop cherries. Fold in two-thirds of cherries to prepared cake batter.

Spread in prepared 9-inch round cake dish. Place on rack or inverted bowl in oven. MW PL5 for 6 minutes, rotating ¼ turn every 3 minutes. Then MW FP 4 - 7 minutes, or until wooden pick inserted in center comes out clean. Let cake stand directly on counter or wooden board 5 minutes to complete cooking. Invert cake onto serving plate. Refrigerate until completely cool. Slice lengthwise to make 2 layers. Set aside. In large chilled bowl, beat whipping cream at high speed until slightly thickened. Add

4 tabelspoons of cherry juice, one at a time, beating until thickened. Spread bottom cake layer with one-third whipped cream mixture. Spread remaining cherries gently over whipped cream layer. Top with remaining cake layer. Frost top and sides of cake with remaining whipped cream. Place semi-sweet chocolate in small bowl. MW FP 1½ - 2 minutes, or until melted. Drizzle over cake. Refrigerate until serving.

APPLESAUCE CAKE

1 c. packed brown sugar
½ c. margarine or butter
1 egg
1 c. unsweetened applesauce
1¼ c. all-purpose flour
1 tsp. ground cinnamon

½ tsp. baking soda
½ tsp. salt
½ tsp. ground cloves
½ tsp. ground nutmeg
½ tsp. ground allspice
½ c. raisins

Lightly grease 8 - 10 cup baking ring. Beat brown sugar and margarine until smooth. Beat egg. Stir in applesauce. Mix in flour, cinnamon, baking soda, salt, cloves, nutmeg and allspice. Stir in raisins.

Pour batter into baking ring. MW PL7 for 4 minutes. MW FP until wooden pick inserted in center comes out clean, 4 - 5 minutes. Cool 5 minutes. Invert onto serving plate. YIELD: 1 cake.

CARROT CAKE WITH CREAM CHEESE FROSTING

1½ c. flour	3 eggs
1½ tsp. baking powder	2 c. grated, raw carrots
1¼ tsp. baking soda	10 oz. can crushed pineapple, drained very well
¾ tsp. salt	
2 tsp. cinnamon	½ c. chopped walnuts or pecans
1½ c. white sugar	
1 c. vegetable oil	

CREAM CHEESE FROSTING:

¼ c. butter	2 c. icing sugar
4 oz. cream cheese	1 tsp. vanilla

Sift together dry ingredients. Beat sugar, oil and eggs together until light colored and well blended. Add dry ingredients and mix well. Stir in carrots, drained pineapple and nuts. Pour into 10 - 12 cup bundt pan, cover and MW PL6 for 10 minutes. MW FP 5 minutes. Cover with foil and let stand 5 - 10 minutes. Remove foil; let stand 5 minutes. Remove from pan and let cool. When cool, frost with Cream Cheese Frosting. YIELD: 12 - 16 servings.

FROSTING: Put butter and cream cheese into a bowl and MW PL3 for 30 - 45 seconds to soften. DO NOT MELT. Add icing sugar and vanilla and mix with a wooden spoon until well mixed and smooth.

CHERRY AMARETTO CAKE

1 pouch white cake mix	1½ c. cherry pie filling
1 egg	Sliced, toasted almonds
½ tsp. almond extract	Red food color
1 env. whipped topping mix or	Amaretto liqueur
1 c. whipping cream	

Mix batter with egg and water as called for on package, reducing water by 2 tablespoons. Pour all except ½ cup of batter into a ring mold. Add a few drops of red food color to reserved batter and stir to blend. Marble red batter into white batter in mold.

Cover with waxed paper. MW PL6 for 5 minutes then MW FP 2 minutes. Let stand, covered, for 5 minutes. Turn out onto serving plate. Pierce top of cake with a skewer and sprinkle cake with Amaretto. Let cake cool completely.

Prepare whipped topping mix according to package directions but use almond extract instead of vanilla, or whip whipping cream and add almond extract to it. Tint a light pink using a drop of red food color, if desired.

Frost cooled cake with cream. Pour cherry pie filling in center hole. Garnish with toasted, sliced almonds. Slice cake and spoon a few cherries onto each serving. YIELD: 8 - 10 servings.

CHOCOLATE ZUCCHINI CAKE

1¼	c. unsifted all-purpose flour	1	c. sugar
¼	c. cocoa	2	eggs
1	tsp. baking powder	1	tsp. vanilla
¾	tsp. baking soda	1	tsp. orange zest
½	tsp. salt	1	c. coarsely grated zucchini
½	tsp. cinnamon	¼	c. milk
6	tbsp. soft butter	½	c. chopped nuts

GLAZE:

1	tbsp. melted butter	1½	tbsp. orange juice
1	c. icing sugar		

Sift first six ingredients together. Beat butter, sugar and orange zest together. Beat in eggs, one at a time, until fluffy. Stir in vanilla, and zucchini. Add to dry ingredients alternately with milk. Stir in nuts. Pour batter into 2-quart ring mold or a casserole dish with an upright glass standing in the centre of it. Elevate off oven floor on a rack or inverted saucer. MW PL5 for 10 minutes. Let stand 10 minutes on a flat surface, covered, to finish cooking. Turn out of pan to cool.

Put butter in a 2-cup measure. MW FP 30 seconds or until melted. Add icing sugar and orange juice and mix until no lumps remain. Drizzle over cake.

CHOCOLATE APPLESAUCE CAKE

½	c. oil	½	tsp. nutmeg
2	oz. semi-sweet baking chocolate	¼	tsp. cloves
2	c. flour	¼	tsp. salt
1	c. sugar	½	c. raisins
½	tbsp. cornstarch	1	c. chopped nuts
2	tsp. baking soda	14	oz. can applesauce
1	tsp. cinnamon		Icing sugar

Combine oil and chocolate in small heat-resistant bowl. MW FP, uncovered, 1½ minutes or until chocolate is melted. Set aside.

Stir together flour, sugar, cornstarch, soda, cinnamon, nutmeg, cloves, salt, raisins and nuts in a medium-size bowl. Add chocolate mixture and applesauce. Mix until well blended.

Pour into 7 x 12 inch baking dish. Elevate dish on rack or inverted bowl. MW FP, uncovered, 12 - 13 minutes or until a wooden toothpick inserted in the centre comes out clean. Turn dish 3 to 4 times during the cooking process.

Allow the cake to cool on a wooden board. Before serving, dust with sifted icing sugar. YIELD: 10 - 12 servings.

COOL AND CREAMY CHEESECAKE

¼	c. butter	1	tbsp. gelatin
1 ¼	c. fine graham wafer crumbs	¼	c. water
		1	tsp. vanilla or
2	tbsp. sugar	¼	c. lemon juice
2	egg yolks, beaten	1	lb. cream cheese, softened
³/₈	c. sugar	2	eggs whites
¹/₈	tsp. salt	¼	c. sugar
¼	c. milk	½	c. whipping cream

Place butter in 9-inch pie plate. MW FP 45 seconds, until melted. Blend in crumbs and sugar. Press firmly and evenly into bottom and sides of dish to form crust. MW FP 2 - 2½ minutes, rotating dish ½ turn after 1 minute. Cool. In 1½-quart casserole beat eggs, sugar and salt until very well blended and light in colour. Place milk in glass measure. MW FP 1 minute, or until scalded. Gradually add to egg mixture stirring well. Cover with casserole lid. MW PL3 for 6 - 8 minutes, stirring after 3 minutes, until thickened. Soak gelatin in water. Add gelatin to hot custard and stir until dissolved. Cool. Add vanilla or lemon juice. Beat cream cheese until smooth. Gradually beat the custard into the cheese until well blended. Whip egg whites until fluffy. Add sugar gradually, continue beating until stiff but not dry. Fold into cheese mixture. Pour into crust. Sprinkle with reserved crumbs if desired. Chill 3 - 4 hours before serving. Serve with Raspberry Sauce.

RASPBERRY SAUCE

2	tbsp. cornstarch	15	oz. pkg. frozen raspberries, thawed
¼	c. sugar		
⅛	tsp. salt		

In 1-quart casserole, stir together cornstarch, sugar and salt. Stir in raspberries. MW FP 5 - 7 minutes, sitrring every 2 minutes, until sauce is thickened and clear. YIELD: 1½ cups.

DUMP CAKE

2 -	22 oz. cans pie filling	4	tbsp. brown sugar
19	oz. (approx.) golden cake mix	2	tsp. cinnamon
		½	c. chopped nuts
½	c. cold margarine or butter		

Dump pie filling into a 9 x 13 inch glass baking dish. Shake to distribute evenly. Dump dry cake mix over pie filling. Slice butter thinly and place thin slices over cake mix. Combine sugar, cinnamon and nuts. Sprinkle mixture over butter. Cover dish with waxed paper. MW FP 15 minutes. Let stand, covered, 10 minutes. YIELD: 12 - 16 servings.

DARK JEWELLED FRUITCAKE

3 c. chopped pitted dates
3 c. pecan or walnut halves,
    or a combination
10 oz. jar red maraschino
    cherry halves
6 oz. jar whole green
    maraschino cherries
¾ c. all-purpose flour
¾ c. brown sugar, packed

½ tsp. nutmeg
½ tsp. baking powder
½ tsp. salt
3 eggs
1 tsp. vanilla
¼ c. fine graham cracker
    crumbs (about 4 square
    crackers)
¼ c. brandy, optional

In large mixing bowl, combine dates, nuts, cherries, flour, sugar, nutmeg, baking powder, salt, eggs and vanilla. Mixture will initially be stiff, but will soften as it is mixed.

Grease an 8 - 12 cup microwave tube or bundt pan and coat with crumbs. Pour batter into pan and place pan in oven on rack, inverted saucer or inverted baking dish.

MW PL5 rotating ¼ turn every 5 minutes until cake begins to pull away from sides of pan, 25 - 30 minutes. Place cake, in pan, directly on heatproof counter or wooden board (not on cooling rack) for 15 minutes, then unmold. Let cool completely.

Drizzle cake with brandy, if desired. Wrap in double thickness of plastic wrap or in aluminum foil and freeze or store in refrigerator no longer than 4 weeks. Serves 10 or more.

FRUITCAKE

½ c. diced candied green
    cherries
½ c. diced candied red cherries
½ c. chopped citron
½ c. golden raisins
½ c. chopped dates
¼ c. currants
⅓ c. brandy
½ c. packed dark brown
    sugar
½ c. margarine or butter

1 tsp. vanilla
3 eggs
2 tbsp. molasses
¾ c. all-purpose flour
½ tsp. salt
½ tsp. baking powder
½ tsp. ground nutmeg
½ tsp. ground allspice
1 c. coarsely chopped
    walnuts

Lightly grease 8 - 10 cup baking ring. Mix green and red cherries, citron, raisins, dates, currants and brandy. Set aside. Beat brown sugar, margarine and vanilla until fluffy; add eggs and molasses. Beat in remaining ingredients except nuts until well blended. Stir in fruit and brandy mixture and nuts. Pour into baking ring. Elevate ring on rack or inverted bowl.

MW PL7 until wooden pick inserted in center comes out clean, 10 - 16 minutes. Rotate 2 or 3 times. Let stand 5 minutes; remove from baking ring. Cool. Wrap in cheesecloth which has been dampened with wine or brandy, if desired. Wrap tightly in plastic wrap and then foil wrap. It is best to "ripen" one week before serving.

I SCREAM FOR ICE CREAM CONES

1½ c. flour
1   c. white sugar
3   tbsp. cocoa
½   tsp. baking powder
½   tsp. baking soda

½   tsp. salt
1   c. water
Flat bottomed ice cream cone cups

HOLE #1: 1 tbsp. vinegar
HOLE #2: 5 tbsp. melted margarine
HOLE #3: 1 tsp. vanilla

Mix all the dry ingredients in a bowl. Make 3 holes (like when you are building sand castles) in the dry ingredients. Put the margarine in a glass measuring cup and MW FP 1 minute to melt. Fill each hole as shown. Pour the water over the whole works and stir to mix well. Put 2 tablespoons of batter in each ice cream cone cup. Fill 8 cones. Set in a doughnut pattern on oven floor and MW FP 3½ - 4 minutes. When cool frost.

LIGHT COCONUT FRUITCAKE

¼   c. butter, melted
1   c. shredded coconut
1   c. all-purpose flour

1¼ c. sugar
½   tsp. baking powder
4   eggs, beaten

2   c. chopped mixed candied fruit
1   c. chopped pecans

¼   c. fine graham cracker crumbs
½   c. orange juice

In large mixing bowl, combine butter, coconut, flour, 1 cup sugar, baking powder, eggs, fruit and nuts. Mix to blend. Mixture will initially be stiff, but will soften as it is mixed.

Grease an 8 - 12 cup microwave tube or bundt pan and coat with crumbs.

Pour batter into pan and place pan in oven on rack, inverted saucer or inverted baking dish. MW PL5 rotating ¼ turn every 5 minutes, until cake begins to pull away from sides of pan, 25 - 30 minutes.

Place cake, in pan, directly on heatproof counter or wooden board (not on cooling rack) and cool 15 minutes, then unmold. Stir together orange juice and remaining sugar in 1-quart measuring cup.

MW FP 3 - 6 minutes, until boiling in all areas and sugar is dissolved. Spoon onto cake. Cool cake completely. Wrap cake in double thickness of plastic wrap or in aluminum foil, freeze or store in refrigerator no longer than 4 weeks. Serves 10 or more.

MELBA CHEESECAKE

¼ c. butter or margarine	⅓ c. sugar
1¼ c. graham cracker crumbs	½ c. sour cream
2 tbsp. sugar	1 egg
16 oz. can sliced peaches, drained	½ tsp. almond extract
	⅓ c. raspberry jam
8 oz. pkg. cream cheese	

Put butter in pie plate. MW FP 45 seconds or until melted. Mix in crumbs and 2 tablespoons sugar; press onto bottom and sides of pie plate. MW FP 1½ - 2 minutes or until hot. Arrange peaches on crust.

Put cream cheese in bowl. MW PL5 for 1 minute or until soft. Blend in remaining ingredients, except jam; pour over peaches. MW FP 3½ - 4½ minutes or until edges are set, rotating once. Cool. Spoon jam onto pie, spread to cover. Refrigerate until served.

"ONE BOWL" WHITE CAKE

1¾ c. sifted cake flour	½ c. soft shortening
2½ tsp. baking powder	½ tsp. vanilla
½ tsp. salt	¾ c. milk
1 c. sugar	2 eggs

Sift together flour, baking powder, salt and sugar in medium-size bowl. Add shortening, vanilla and two-thirds of the milk. Beat vigorously for 2 minutes at medium speed. Add remaining milk and eggs. Beat 2 minutes more. Batter should be smooth.

Pour batter into 9-inch microware cake pan (2½ inches deep). Elevate on rack or inverted bowl. MW FP 8 minutes, giving cake a ¼ turn every 2 minutes. YIELD: 9-inch layer cake.

TRIPLE CHOCOLATE BUNDT CAKE

19 oz. pkg. deep chocolate cake mix (2-layer)	1 c. water
	½ c. oil
6 oz. pkg. instant chocolate pudding mix	4 eggs
	Icing sugar
½ c. chocolate syrup	

Thoroughly grease 10-inch microwave tube pan or bundt pan. Combine cake mix, pudding mix, syrup, water and oil in large mixer bowl. Beat at medium speed for 2 minutes, or until smooth. Add eggs one at a time, beating after each addition. Pour mixture into pan. Elevate pan. MW FP 11 - 14 minutes, rotating dish ¼ turn every 5 minutes. Let stand upright in pan 30 minutes. Loosen and remove from pan. Sprinkle cooled cake with sifted icing sugar, or frost as desired.

ORANGE/PINEAPPLE CHEESECAKE

⅓ c. butter	2 eggs
2 c. graham cracker crumbs	½ c. orange juice
1 tbsp. sugar	concentrate, thawed
¼ tsp. salt	Pineapple-Orange Glaze
2 - 8 oz. pkgs. cream cheese, softened	Maraschino cherries with stems (optional)
½ c. sugar	

Put butter in deep, 9-inch, glass pie plate. MW FP 40 seconds or until melted. Mix in graham cracker crumbs, sugar and salt. Press into pie plate. MW FP 1¾ minutes. Beat cream cheese in large mixer bowl. Add eggs and ½ cup sugar. Beat until smooth. Add orange juice concentrate. Pour into crust. MW FP 6 minutes. Spread Orange/Pineapple Glaze over hot pie. Chill at least 8 hours in refrigerator. Garnish with maraschino cherries, if desired.

ORANGE/PINEAPPLE GLAZE

½ c. sugar	½ c. water
¼ c. flour	1 - 14½ oz. can crushed
¼ c. orange juice concentrate, thawed	pineapple, drained

In 4-cup glass liquid measuring cup, blend sugar and flour. Combine water and concentrate. Stir into sugar mixture. MW FP 2½ minutes (stir every 30 seconds). Stir in pineapple. YIELD: 6 servings.

PINEAPPLE UPSIDE DOWN CAKE

¼ c. butter	6 maraschino cherries
½ c. brown sugar	1 pouch golden cake mix
6 pineapple rings	1 egg

Put butter in 9-inch round cake dish. MW FP 45 seconds or until melted.

Add brown sugar and stir to blend. Spread evenly on bottom of plate. Reserve juice from pineapple and put 6 rings down over the sugar mixture in the cake pan. Put a cherry in the hole of each pineapple ring. Mix the cake mix using the reserved pineapple juice instead of the water called for, reducing the liquid by 25 per cent, and the egg. Pour cake batter carefully over pineapple.

Cover with waxed paper. MW PL6 for 6 minutes. Turn dish ½ turn if necessary and MW FP 3 minutes. Let stand, covered, 5 minutes. Invert onto serving dish. YIELD: 8 servings.

MANDARIN RING CAKE

Use Pineapple Upside Down Cake recipe but substitute mandarin orange segments in place of pineapple and juice from oranges instead of pineapple juice. Also, if you have a ring pan it can be used. If not, a regular cake dish will do. As an added touch, after inverting onto serving plate, sprinkle with Grand Marnier.

PRALINE 'N' PECAN CAKE

½ c. raisins	½ c. hot water
1 - 10 oz. pkg. traditional white frosting	½ c. ground pecans
	1 c. unsifted all-purpose flour
½ tsp. salt	
1 ½ tsp. rum extract	1 c. sugar
2 tsp. baking powder	1 tsp. cinnamon
3 eggs, beaten	½ c. butter or margarine, melted
⅓ c. evaporated milk	

Place raisins in small dish and cover with hot water. MW FP 30 seconds. Set aside. Stir together frosting mix, flour, sugar, baking powder, salt and pecans. Add eggs, butter, milk and rum extract. Mix well. Drain raisins and stir into batter. Pour into greased 12 x 8 x 2 inch dish. MW FP 16 minutes, giving dish ½ turn after 8 minutes. Frost immediately with Praline Frosting. (see page 83)

PUMPKIN CHEESECAKE

3 tbsp. margarine or butter	¾ c. packed brown sugar
1 c. fine graham cracker crumbs	3 eggs
	1½ tbsp. all-purpose flour
¼ c. granulated or packed brown sugar	1 tsp. ground cinnamon
	½ tsp. ground nutmeg
8 oz. pkg. cream cheese	½ tsp. vanilla
1 c. canned pumpkin	

Place margarine in 9-inch pie plate. MW FP until melted, 30 seconds - 1 minute. Add graham cracker crumbs and sugar, mix thoroughly. Press mixture firmly against bottom and side of pie plate.

MW PL7 until hot, 2 - 4 minutes. Rotate pie plate once or twice during cooking. Cool completely before filling.

Place cream cheese in medium bowl. MW PL5 until softened, 1 - 2 minutes. Add remaining ingredients. Beat at medium speed of electric mixer until smooth and well blended.

MW PL7 until hot and thickened, 6 - 8 minutes, stirring every 2 minutes. Pour into crust. MW PL5 until filling is firm to the touch, 10 - 15 minutes. Center may appear soft-set. Garnish with pecan halves, if desired. Refrigerate until set. YIELD: 9-inch pie.

PRALINE FROSTING

¾ c. brown sugar (packed)   ¾ c. sugar
⅓ c. evaporated milk   ¾ c. chopped pecans

Combine brown sugar, sugar and milk. Stir in pecans. Pour mixture over hot cake. MW FP 4 minutes, giving dish ½ turn after 2 minutes. Serve warm or cool.

SEVEN-UP CAKE WITH PINEAPPLE TOPPING

BATTER:
19 oz. pkg. yellow cake mix   4   eggs
4   oz. pkg. instant vanilla   ¾   c. cooking oil
    pudding   1¼ c. (10 oz.) 7-Up drink
1   c. flaked coconut

TOPPING:
¼ c. butter or margarine   1   c. (8 oz.) crushed pine ple,
3 eggs   undrained
1 c. sugar

Place butter in a 1-quart casserole. MW FP 30 - 45 seconds or until melted. Stir in eggs and sugar. MW FP 4 - 6 minutes or until thickened. Stir occasionally. Stir in pineapple. Set aside. Mix together all batter ingredients except 7-Up in a large mixing bowl until well blended. Stir in 7-Up. Pour batter into an 11¾ x 7½ x 1¾ inch baking dish. Tap bottom gently.

Cover with a paper towel. Elevate dish. MW PL7 for 16 - 18 minutes or until a cake tester inserted near center comes out clean. Turn dish a half turn halfway through cooking. Immediately remove paper towel and spread topping over cake. Allow to stand 5 - 10 minutes on a solid surface. YIELD: 12 - 16 servings.

HINT:

— *To clean oven, MW a soaking wet cloth or sponge FP 3 minutes. The steam will loosen any baked on foods. Wipe out oven with dry cloth.*

WALNUT CARROT CAKE

1½ c. sugar	¾ tsp. salt
1 c. oil	1¼ tsp. baking soda
1 tsp. vanilla	2½ tsp. cinnamon
3 eggs	2¼ c. raw grated carrots
1½ c. flour	½ c. ground walnuts

Grease tube pan in accordance with manufacturer's directions (some manufacturers say not to). If you do not have a tube pan a 12 x 8 inch will do.

In large bowl blend together sugar, oil and vanilla. Add eggs. Beat well. In small bowl combine flour, salt, soda and cinnamon. Mix well.

Add flour mixture to sugar mixture. Mix thoroughly. Fold in carrots and walnuts. Spread batter in prepared pan.

Elevate pan on rack or inverted bowl. MW PL6 for 10 minutes, then MW FP 8 - 10 minutes. Turn the dish ¼ turn every 4 minutes or until cake tests done.

Remove cake from oven and place on counter or wooden board to cool (as the heat will be retained near the bottom of the cake and ensure that the bottom of the cake is cooked). Frost with Creamy Cheese Icing, if desired.

CREAMY CHEESE ICING

| 2½ c. icing sugar | 6 tbsp. butter |
| 1 - 8 oz. pkg. cream cheese | 2 tsp. vanilla |

Place sugar on bottom of a 2-quart casserole dish. Place remaining ingredients on top. MW FP 1 minute. Beat well with an electric mixer until light and fluffy.

HINT:

— *Heat baby oil in MW for a few seconds to warm and rub into sore muscles.*

CLASSY CANDY - HOW TO MICROWAVE

Unless otherwise specified, the chocolate "wafers" referred to in the recipes are not pure chocolate, but a compounded chocolate in which the cocoa butter has been removed and replaced with coconut or palm oil. The reason for this is because cocoa butter is very temperamental and requires a special, time consuming tempering process. Chocolate compound wafers do not require this treatment and make candy making quick and convenient, without the extra tempering process.

Wafers are available in bulk food stores, candy shops, cake decorating supply stores and even in some hobby shops. They come in various colors and even varying qualities. The price is somewhat of a clue as to the quality, but before you make a major purchase, buy a few for taste testing. The creamier, richer and more deeply flavored, the better quality the wafers are.

If wafers become thickened while you are working with them, you can thin them by reheating and adding one tablespoon per pound of vegetable shortening, i.e. Crisco. Lard, oil, butter or milk will only cause the mixture to seize further.

Water is an enemy of the wafers and that is why microwaving is a far better method for melting them than over hot water.

Special flavoring oils are available where you purchase the wafers. Liquids, like extracts, which are alcohol based, will cause the melted compound to thicken and seize. The oils are to be used very sparingly.

Chocolate chips and baking chocolate can be treated in the same manner as the wafers. Chocolate holds its shape, even when melted in the microwave; be sure to stir it often.

Microwaves are readily attracted to fats and sugars. They will be very hot in a short time. Be careful in handling.

ALMOND BARK

1   c. whole almonds   1   lb. white coating wafers
    (not blanched)
    dotted with 1 tsp. butter

Put nuts in a ring fashion in a pie plate. MW FP 5 minutes, stirring and checking after every minute. Nuts should be golden brown.

Put wafers in a 4-cup measure. MW FP 2 - 4 minutes to melt, stirring after each minute. Add toasted nuts.

Line a cookie sheet with waxed paper. Pour bark onto prepared pan. Let set at room temperature. When set, break into serving pieces.

BAKED WALNUTS

1 lb. walnuts	½ c. butter or margarine
1 c. brown sugar	1 tsp. cinnamon

Put butter in 4-cup measure. MW FP 1 minute or until melted. Mix in cinnamon and sugar. MW FP 2 minutes or until sugar is dissolved. Add nuts. MW FP 3 - 5 minutes longer or until nuts are hot and bubbly. Let cool a few minutes, then turn out on waxed paper to dry. Store in airtight container. YIELD: 1 pound.

BAVARIAN MINTS

1 can sweetened condensed milk (1⅓ cups)	1 lb. white wafers with 5 drops of oil of peppermint added
1 lb. mint flavored green wafers or	

Butter a 9 x 13 inch pan. Line with waxed paper. Butter waxed paper. Put wafers into a 4-cup measure and MW FP 2 - 4 minutes, stirring after every minute until wafers are melted. Add sweetened condensed milk. MW FP 30 seconds. Stir well to blend. Pour into prepared pan. When almost set, cut into small squares using a knife dipped in hot water and dried. Dip cut squares in melted dark chocolate coating.

BUTTERSCOTCH ROCKY ROAD

2 c. semi-sweet chocolate chips	10½ oz. pkg. miniature marshmallows
2 c. butterscotch chips	1 c. salted peanuts
1 c. peanut butter	

Combine chocolate chips, butterscotch chips and peanut butter in a large glass mixing bowl. MW PL7 for 5 minutes, uncovered. Stir until melted. Fold in marshmallows and peanuts. Butter a 9 x 13 inch pan, line with waxed paper, butter waxed paper. Pour mixture into prepared pan. Refrigerate until set. Cut into squares.

CARAMEL POPCORN

5 c. popped corn	½ c. light corn syrup
1 c. brown sugar	¾ tsp. baking soda
½ c. butter	

Put brown sugar, butter and corn syrup in a bowl. MW FP 1 - 2 minutes or until melted. MW FP 3½ minutes. Add baking soda. Put popcorn in a large casserole. Pour syrup mixture over popcorn. Stir and/or shake well to coat. MW FP 1½ minutes. Stir popcorn mixture. MW FP 1½ minutes. Stir popcorn mixture. MW FP ½ minute. Stir. Pour onto cookie sheet to cool.

CHOCOLATEY PEANUT BUTTER FUDGE

1 c. peanut butter flavored chips
2 c. semi-sweet chocolate chips
14 oz. can sweetened condensed milk
¼ c. butter
1 c. chopped peanuts

Place all ingredients in a LARGE bowl. MW PL5 for 3 - 5 minutes, stirring once or twice, until all the chips are melted. Stir in nuts. Pour into buttered 8 x 8 inch pan. Refrigerate until set. YIELD: 2 pounds.

EASIEST EVER MICROWAVE FUDGE

4 c. icing sugar
½ c. cocoa (unsweetened)
½ c. butter
¼ c. evaporated milk
2 tsp. vanilla
¾ c. chopped pecans
¾ c. chopped maraschino cherries (drained DRY)

Sieve icing sugar together with cocoa in a large casserole. Cut butter into chunks and sprinkle on mixture. Pour evaporated (NOT CONDENSED) milk over mixture. MW FP 2½ minutes. Add vanilla, pecans and cherries. Mix well. Butter an 8 x 8 inch pan. Line with waxed paper. Butter waxed paper. Pour fudge into prepared pan. Put in fridge to set. Will set in freezer in about 10 minutes if you are in a hurry. Cut into small squares.

GRANOLA CRUNCH

¼ c. butter
⅜ c. packed brown sugar
⅛ c. honey
⅛ c. water
½ tsp. salt
½ tsp. cinnamon
1½ c. old fashioned oats
½ c. sunflower seeds or almond slices
½ c. wheat germ

In a 2-quart casserole combine butter, sugar, honey, water, salt and cinnamon. MW FP 2½ - 4 minutes, or until slightly thickened, stirring after 2 minutes.

Stir in remaining ingredients. MW PL5 for 4 - 6 minutes or until rich golden brown, stirring after 2 minutes, then every 2 minutes. Spread on buttered cookie sheet, pressing down lightly with spatula. Let stand until firm. Break into smaller pieces and store in airtight container.

HINT:

— *Heat baby's bottle in MW. Be sure to shake halfway through and after heating.*

MICROWAVE CARAMELS

2	c. sugar	1	c. light corn syrup
1	c. butter	1	tsp. vanilla
1	can sweetened condensed milk	1	c. chopped nuts

Combine sugar, butter and corn syrup in a 3-quart casserole. MW FP 5 minutes or until butter is melted. Stir mixture to dissolve sugar. GRADUALLY blend in sweetened condensed milk (IF ADDED TOO QUICKLY OR ALL AT ONCE MIXTURE WILL SEPARATE). MW FP 15 - 17 minutes or until 240° F., stirring 4 or 5 times during cooking and checking temperature during last few minutes. Stir in vanilla and nuts. Butter a 9 x 13 inch pan. Pour mixture into prepared pan. Cool. Cut into squares to serve. Can be dipped in melted chocolate.

MICROWAVE FUDGE

2	c. white sugar	10	lge. marshmallows
⅔	c. evaporated milk (NOT condensed milk)	1	c. semi-sweet chocolate chips
½	c. butter	1	c. chopped nuts

Put sugar, milk and butter in a LARGE bowl. Stir to blend. MW FP 4 minutes, stirring once during cooking time. MW FP 5 minutes without stirring. While mixture is cooking, butter an 8 x 8 inch pan, line with waxed paper and butter waxed paper. You also may wish to cut marshmallows in half for quicker melting. Add marshmallows, chocolate chips and nuts and stir until both marshmallows and chocolate chips are melted. Pour into prepared pan. Cool until set. Cut with a sharp knife. YIELD: not enough.

MICROWAVE PEANUT BRITTLE

1	c. white sugar	1	tsp. butter or margarine
½	c. clear corn syrup	1	tsp. vanilla
1	c. salted peanuts	1	tsp. baking soda

Before starting, butter a cookie sheet so it will be ready when needed. Combine sugar and corn syrup in a large bowl. MW FP 3 - 5 minutes until mixture is light brown. Add butter and vanilla, stir to blend. Add peanuts, stir to blend. MW FP 1 - 2 minutes. Peanuts will be brown and syrup hot, so use oven mitts and be careful. Add soda and stir until mixture is light and foamy. Work quickly, as once the soda is added and foams, the mixture will start to set. Pour onto prepared cookie sheet. Let cool ½ hour at room temperature and break into pieces. YIELD: a whole bunch.

MINT SANDWICHES

1	lb. chocolate flavored wafers	2	tbsp. vegetable shortening (hydrogenated) or coconut oil (DIVIDED)
2	c. green or white tinted green wafers	2 - 3	drops oil of peppermint

Put chocolate flavored wafers in a 4-cup measure. MW FP 2 - 4 minutes, stirring after every minute until melted. Add 1 table-spoon of shortening. Put green wafers in a 4-cup measure and MW FP 2 - 4 minutes, stirring after every minute until melted. Add 1 tablespoon of shortening and oil of peppermint. Cool both to 85 - 90⁰ F.

Thinly spread half of the chocolate on a waxed paper lined cookie sheet. Put in fridge to set. When "almost" firm spread with all the green coating. Put in fridge to set. When green layer is firm, spread with remaining chocolate. Let set at room temperature. When set, cut with a sharp knife which has been dipped in hot water and dried. If either of the coatings get too cold while waiting for the last layer to set, MW FP 15 - 20 seconds. Be sure to remove thermometer when putting in MW.

You can substitute the green layer with a pink layer using oil of wintergreen, or white with oil of mint or oil of spearmint. You can stack several layers. Use your imagination!

NOEL FUDGE

1	lb. white coating wafers	1	c. candied green cherries (glace)
1	can sweetened condensed milk	1	c. walnuts or pecans
1	c. red candied cherries		

Put wafers in a 4-cup measure. MW FP 2 - 4 minutes to melt, stirring after each minute. Add sweetened condensed milk and stir to blend well. MW FP 30 seconds. Stir to blend well. Add cherries and nuts. Stir to blend well. Butter a cookie sheet. Line with waxed paper. Butter waxed paper. Pour fudge mixture onto prepared pan. Spread evenly. Chill in fridge for 15 - 20 minutes to set. Cut with a knife dipped in hot water and dried.

NUT CLUSTERS

1	lb. shelled, blanched nuts	1	lb. chocolate flavored wafers

Put nuts (peanuts, cashews, filberts, hazelnuts or a combination thereof) into a pie plate in a doughnut fashion. MW FP 5 minutes, checking and stirring after every minute to brown nuts. Put wafers into a 5-cup measure and MW FP 2 - 4 minutes, stirring after every minute until melted. Add nuts. Let stand 5 minutes. Line a cookie sheet with waxed paper. Put spoonfuls of nut mixture onto waxed paper to make clusters. Let set at room temperature. When hardened, peel off waxed paper.

PEANUT BUTTER FUDGE

2	c. white granulated sugar	10	lge. marshmallows
⅔	c. evaporated milk	1	tsp. vanilla
1	c. peanut butter (chunky)		

Combine sugar and evaporated milk in a LARGE MW safe bowl. MW FP 4½ - 5 minutes, uncovered, until mixture begins to boil, stirring after 3 minutes. MW FP 5 minutes. Do NOT stir. Stir in peanut butter, marshmallows and vanilla and mix until well blended and all marshmallows are melted. Pour into a buttered 8 x 8 inch pan. Cool until set. Cut into squares.

SUGAR 'N' SPICE NUTS

2	tbsp. butter	¼	tsp. nutmeg
¼	c. packed brown sugar	1	tbsp. water
½	tsp. cinnamon	2	c. shelled walnuts, pecan
¼	tsp. salt		halves or whole almonds

Put butter in a 1-quart casserole. MW FP 1 minute or until melted. Add remaining ingredients. Stir until nuts are coated evenly. MW uncovered FP 4 - 5 minutes or until nuts are toasted and glazed, stirring after 2, 3 and 4 minutes. Spoon nuts into a single layer onto a waxed paper lined cookie sheet to cool.

TRUFFLES IN CHOCOLATE CUPS - DECADENT

Make "cups" using tiny paper bon bon cups as molds by coating with at least two layers of melted semi-sweet chocolate chips. Chill. Remove paper. Fill with the following:

2	tbsp. butter	4	oz. semi-sweet chocolate
4	oz. milk chocolate chopped		chips
	into small pieces	⅛	tsp. salt
	(Jersey Milk is okay)	½	tsp. peppermint extract
2	eggs		

Put butter in a 4-cup measure. MW FP 2 minutes until bubbly and foamy. Add chopped chocolate and chocolate chips. Stir until melted and smooth. If necessary return to MW 30 - 45 seconds to melt chocolate.

In a small bowl beat eggs and salt until foamy and lemon colored, using an electric mixer. On high speed very gradually add warm chocolate mixture. Mixture should be about the thickness of mayonnaise. Stir in peppermint extract.

Fill chocolate cups. These freeze well in a sealed container. To serve, bring to room temperature, keeping in sealed container while thawing to prevent condensation from forming on them as they defrost.

TRUFFLES

My friend Brenda is not what one might call your typical Suzie Homemaker type, but witty, she is. When asked if she had any wittiness for this cook book she said . . . No, I don't have any wittiness, but I do have a great recipe.

12 oz. pkg. semi-sweet chocolate chips	1 tsp. vanilla
1 c. ground walnuts	Dash salt
¾ c. sweetened condensed milk	Shredded coconut, chopped nuts or powdered sugar

Place chocolate chips in medium sized bowl. MW PL7 until melted, 2 - 4 minutes, stirring twice. Stir in walnuts, condensed milk, vanilla and salt. Cool 5 minutes.

Shape into ¾ - 1 inch balls. Dip into coconut, chopped nuts or powdered sugar. Place on greased baking sheet and refrigerate until set. YIELD: 50 - 60 pieces.

HINT:

— *To remove plastic wrap from frozen foods, MW FP until wrapper looks moist.*

SWEETENED CONDENSED MILK SUBSTITUTE

⅔ c. butter or margarine	2 c. dry skim milk powder (do not reconstitute)
⅔ c. hot water	
1½ c. granulated sugar	

Put butter in a large microproof bowl. MW FP 1 minute or until melted. Gently stir in hot water. Stir dry skim milk powder and sugar together. Add to butter mixture. MW FP 3½ - 5 minutes or until mixture boils, whisking every minute. Cool and refrigerate overnight before using for best results. YIELD: 2 cups.

HINT:

— *To get the last bit of ketchup, etc., remove lid and MW FP 15 - 30 seconds.*

ANOTHER

½ lb. chocolate flavored   Harvest Crunch
     wafers

Put wafers into a 4-cup measure and MW FP 2 - 4 minutes, stirring after every minute until melted. Stir in Harvest Crunch (orange label - without dates and raisins is my favorite, but any granola mixture will do) until mixture is no longer runny. It will be quite stiff to stir. Drop in mounds (approx. 1 tbsp. each) onto a waxed paper lined cookie sheet. Let set at room temperature.

BAR COOKIES

½   c. shortening   2   c. flour
½   c. brown sugar,   ½   tsp. baking soda
     firmly packed   ½   tsp. salt
¼   c. white sugar   6   oz. semi-sweet chocolate
1   tsp. vanilla   chips
1   egg

Press batter into waxed paper lined 9 x 13 inch baking dish. MW PL5 for 8 - 10 minutes or just until dry on the surface. Rotate dish a quarter turn every 2 minutes to avoid overcooking in corners of pan. When surface appears dry, sprinkle chocolate chips on top. MW FP 1 - 3 minutes just until chips are melted. Spread chocolate evenly over surface of cookies. Cool and cut into squares.

CHOCOLATE CRACKLES

¼   c. butter   1   tsp. vanilla
2   oz. unsweetened chocolate   ½   tsp. salt
1   c. white sugar   2   c. flour
2   eggs   Icing sugar
2   tsp. baking powder

Combine butter and chocolate in a bowl. MW PL5 for 1 - 4 minutes, or until melted. Blend well.

Beat in sugar, eggs, baking powder, vanilla and salt. Stir in flour. Refrigerate several hours. Shape dough into 1½ inch balls and roll in icing sugar.

Place 6 - 8 balls in large ring on waxed paper on baking sheet or pie plate. Place one ball in centre of ring. MW PL5 for 1¼ - 3 minutes, or just until surface is dry, rotating every 30 seconds.

Remove waxed paper with cookies on it to countertop. Cool.

CHEWY BROWNIES

½ c. butter
1 c. sugar
1 tsp. vanilla
2 eggs

2 oz. unsweetened baking chocolate
½ c. flour
½ c. chopped walnuts

Cream margarine and sugar. Beat in vanilla. Add eggs. Beat well. MW chocolate FP 1 - 3 minutes or until melted.

Add to egg mixture. Stir in flour and walnuts. Pour into waxed paper lined 8-inch square baking dish. MW FP 3 minutes. Turn dish. MW FP another 3½ minutes.

Let stand 5 minutes, covering dish with layer of waxed paper. Serve plain or with chocolate frosting.

CHOCOLATE MINT BONBONS

¾ c. butter
2 tbsp. green creme de menthe
⅓ c. sugar
⅛ tsp. salt

1¾ c. unsifted all-purpose flour
1 c. chopped pecans
Chocolate fondant topping (recipe follows)

Put butter in microwave mixing bowl. MW PL3 for 45 seconds to soften. Add creme de menthe, sugar and salt.

With electric mixer on medium speed, beat mixture until light and creamy. Stir in flour and pecans.

Form into 1-inch balls and arrange 12 in a circle on microwave baking sheet. MW FP, checking after 2 minutes for done cookies. Remove done cookies and rotate remaining cookies half turn.

Repeat with remaining dough. When cool, top with Chocolate Fondant Topping. YIELD: 48 cookies.

CHOCOLATE FONDANT TOPPING

1 oz. square unsweetened chocolate
1 tbsp. butter
1 tbsp. white corn syrup

1 tbsp. green creme de menthe
1 c. confectioners' sugar
1 tbsp. hot water

Place chocolate in 1-quart microwave bowl. MW PL5, uncovered, 2 - 4 minutes until melted.

Add butter, stirring to melt, then add syrup, creme de menthe and confectioners' sugar.

Stir until smooth. Thin with hot water, if too thick.

CRISPY MARSHMALLOW TREATS

10 oz. pkg. marshmallows
¼ c. butter or margarine
5 c. toasted rice cereal

1 c. salted peanuts
1 c. raisins

Combine marshmallows and butter in large glass bowl. MW FP 3 - 4 minutes, stir twice. Stir until smooth. Add cereal and stir to coat well.

Press into greased 12 x 8 inch dish. Cool; cut into squares to serve. YIELD: 2½ dozen squares.

DON'T TELL ANYONE
HOW EASY THIS IS!

Graham wafers
1 c. butter

1 c. brown sugar
1 c. nuts

This recipe will make one 8 x 8 inch and one 9 x 13 inch pan or one 17 x 11 inch jelly roll pan. There are also two ways to prepare it. One method is to microwave the finished product and the other is to leave it uncooked. Both are delicious. You may wish to experiment the first time you make it and thus it is best to make it in the two dishes the first time. One you can leave uncooked and the other you can cook. If you decide you like the uncooked version, then the next time you can make the recipe in a 17 x 11 inch jelly roll pan. However, if you prefer the cooked version, you will have to make it in the two dishes.

Lay whole graham wafers in bottom of dish(es), being sure to trim wafers to fit the entire bottom of the dish, and being sure to use microproof dishes if you plan to cook it. Sprinkle with toasted almonds (sliced toasted almonds or whole, coarsely chopped toasted almonds, or pecans (my favorite) or walnuts) or your choice of nuts.

Put butter in a 4-cup measure or large bowl. A 4-cup measure with handle is best as the mixture will be very hot and the measuring cup is much easier to get a grip on. MW FP 1 - 2 minutes or until melted. Stir in brown sugar. MW FP 1 minute or until mixture begins to boil. When mixture boils, MW FP 3 minutes, without stirring. Mixture will be very hot and continue to boil even after you remove it from the oven, so be very careful and use oven mitts. Carefully stir the mixture until it is well blended.

Pour evenly over the nut covered graham wafers. At this point you can let the squares cool and cut and serve (my preference) or MW FP until mixture begins to bubble on top of graham wafers, about 1 - 2 minutes. Either way these treats are delicious. Store in an airtight container between sheets of waxed paper.

CHOW MEIN NOODLE NESTS

To quote Cathy, one of my favorite cartoon characters "This dish has been cancelled, I've eaten all the ingredients!!" So, if you can get the batter into the microwave, you're laughing!!

6 oz. pkg. chocolate chips	4 oz. can chow mein noodles
6 oz. pkg. butterscotch chips	7 oz. cocktail peanuts

Melt chocolate and butterscotch chips in a 2½-quart casserole dish in microwave for 4 minutes. Remove. Stir until smooth. Add chow mein noodles and peanuts. Stir until well coated. Drop by teaspoonfuls onto waxed paper. Let set until firm in freezer or refrigerator. YIELD: approx. 4 dozen.

DOUBLE CHOCOLATE BROWNIES

2 eggs	½ tsp. baking powder
⅓ c. vegetable oil	¼ tsp. salt
1 c. white sugar	¼ c. chopped walnuts
1 tsp. vanilla	½ c. semi-sweet chocolate chips
⅔ c. all-purpose flour	
½ c. cocoa	

In medium bowl, beat eggs, oil, sugar and vanilla until well blended. In another bowl, combine flour, cocoa, baking powder and salt. Stir well. Add to egg and sugar mixture; beat well. Pour batter into ungreased 9-inch ring pan. Sprinkle walnuts and chocolate pieces on top. Set pan on top of a rack or inverted bowl in the microwave oven. MW FP 4 - 5 minutes, rotating baking dish one half turn after the first 2 minutes. Brownies will be done when a toothpick inserted comes out with no uncooked batter on it. Cool at least 10 minutes on a solid surface before cutting. YIELD: 20 pieces.

ENERGY BARS

½ c. margarine	¾ c. triticale flour or whole wheat flour
½ c. demerara or brown sugar	½ c. chopped nuts
2 eggs	¼ c. raisins or chopped dates
¼ c. wheat germ	¼ c. flaked coconut

With an electric mixer or a wooden spoon beat margarine until light and fluffy. Cream in sugar. Add eggs and beat well. Mix in flour and wheat germ, then add nuts, raisins and coconut, mixing well. Pour into an 8-inch glass or microwave pan. Elevate on rack or an empty bowl in the microwave oven. This allows for more even, quicker baking of the batter. Cover with waxed paper. MW FP 3½ - 4 minutes. Let stand 5 minutes. Cut into bars when cool. YIELD: 12 bars.

FINDING MR. GOODBAR

This recipe comes from a friend who wishes to remain anonymous, but does have a saying she has borrowed from Garfield the Cat - "Diet is Die with a T!"

1 c. semi-sweet chocolate chips (6 oz.)	1 c. peanut butter
1 c. butterscotch chips (6 oz.)	¼ c. milk
1 c. dry roasted peanuts (approx. 8 oz.)	2 tbsp. dry vanilla pudding
	½ c. butter
	3¼ c. icing sugar
	½ tsp. maple flavoring

Combine chocolate chips, butterscotch chips and peanut butter in a 4-cup measure. MW FP 3 - 3½ minutes, or until softened, stirring after 2 minutes. Stir until melted and blended. Butter a 9 x 13 inch pan. Line with waxed paper. Pour half of the chocolate, butterscotch, peanut butter mixture into the pan. Spread as evenly as possible and then sharply tap the pan on the countertop to finish spreading evenly. Put into freezer for 15 minutes to set.

Stir peanuts into remaining chocolate mixture and allow to stand at room temperature. After base layer has been in the freezer for about 12 minutes, begin preparing the next layer by mixing the milk and dry pudding in a 4-cup measure. Add butter. MW FP 1½ - 2 minutes or until mixture boils. Stir once during cooking.

Stir in icing sugar and maple flavoring. Mix well to blend. Spread over set base layer. Spoon reserved chocolate/peanut mixture over top of the maple layer. Shake and tap pan to spread evenly. Refrigerate until set.

To cut, use a knife dipped in hot water and dried. Remove from pan by lifting out waxed paper liner and cut. Store in fridge.

GINGER COOKIES

¾ c. shortening	2 tsp. soda
1 c. dark brown sugar	½ tsp. salt
¼ c. molasses	1 tsp. ginger
1 egg	1 tsp. ground cinnamon
3 c. flour	1 tsp. ground cloves

Cream together shortening, brown sugar, molasses and egg. Sift together remaining dry ingredients. Stir into creamed mixture. Roll into small balls or drop by teaspoon onto waxed paper. Moisten bottom of a glass and coat with sugar. Lightly press down on each cookie with glass, being careful not to completely flatten. MW PL5 for 5 minutes. YIELD: 5 dozen cookies.

NANAIMO BARS/NEW YORK SLICE

Whether you call them Nanaimo Bars, New York Slice or Pre-menstrual Stress Relief Treats, those decadent dainties from the bridal shower circuit have never been easier or quicker to make. Before Kyle can say "I wanna lick the bowl" I can have this delectable devil in the fridge.

The recipe calls for graham wafer crumbs . . . put graham wafers in the food processor and process until fine, or crush with a rolling pin. My Mother tells me that in the olden days, like the 1970's B.P. (before processors) rolling pins were used to crush crackers to make crumbs! Here I thought they were for flattening dough so you could press little plastic cutters into the dough which either get stuck in the dough or sticks the dough to the counter!

I also remember seeing cartoons of wife-like creatures with murder on their minds bearing rolling pins and chasing husband-like creatures with Cheshire cat-like smiles! Well, I guess if they're good enough for crushing crumbs and skulls of crumbs, then rolling pins will be able to stand in for food processors for making graham wafer crumbs.

Hmmm, I guess processors wouldn't be good for the other type of crumbs though. That's science for you - a giant step forward for mankind and a leap backwards for crumbs!

½	c. butter or margarine	¼	c. butter or margarine
¼	c. sugar	2	tbsp. vanilla custard powder
1	egg		
4	tbsp. unsweetened cocoa powder	2	c. sifted icing sugar
		½	tsp. vanilla extract
2	c. graham wafer crumbs	4	oz. semi-sweet chocolate, chips or squares
1	c. coconut		
½	c. chopped walnuts or pecans	1	tbsp. vegetable shortening NOT LARD

Put butter or margarine in a 4-cup glass measure. MW FP 1 minute or until melted. Whisk in sugar, egg and cocoa. MW FP 1½ minutes, whisking every 30 seconds. Dump crumbs, coconut and nuts into mixture. Blend well. Press into buttered 8 x 12 inch pan. Cool while preparing next layer.

Cream ¼ cup butter or margarine with custard powder, icing sugar and vanilla extract. Spread over mixture in pan. Chill mixture while preparing next layer.

Put chocolate pieces and vegetable shortening in a 4-cup glass measure. MW FP 2 - 3 minutes, stirring every 30 seconds, until melted. Spread over chilled layers in pan.

Score cutting lines with a knife while chocolate is still soft. Use a knife dipped in hot water and dried to cut squares in order not to shatter chocolate topping.

PEANUT BUTTER COOKIES

½ c. butter
½ c. brown sugar
½ c. white sugar
½ c. chunky peanut butter
1 egg, beaten

1½ c. flour
¼ tsp. baking soda
¼ tsp. salt
1 tsp. vanilla

Cream together butter, sugar and peanut butter. Add egg. Blend in flour, baking soda, salt and vanilla. Shape dough into 1½-inch balls. Arrange in circular fashion on waxed paper or microwave-safe baking tray. Space balls 2 inches apart to allow for spreading. Flatten with fork dipped in sugar. MW PL6 for 2½ - 3 minutes. Remove on waxed paper to cool. Microwave remaining cookies using fresh waxed paper each time. Remember that cookies will look slightly doughy and moist when they should be taken from the microwave. They will continue to cook on standing.

PEANUT BUTTER BARS

¾ c. margarine
1 c. brown sugar
1 tsp. vanilla
⅓ c. peanut butter
1 egg, beaten

2 c. flour
1 c. semi-sweet chocolate chips
½ c. peanut butter

Cream margarine until fluffy. Add sugar, vanilla and ⅓ cup peanut butter and continue beating until fluffy. Add egg and beat in well. Add flour and mix well. Divide dough into two equal portions. Press each portion into an 8-inch round baking dish. Cover with waxed paper. Prepare topping by putting chocolate chips and ½ cup peanut butter in a 2-cup measure. MW FP 2 minutes, stirring 2 - 3 times during cooking. Stir well to blend. Set aside. MW each dish FP 3 - 4 minutes, stopping halfway through to rotate dish if necessary. Cover with topping and let stand, covered with dish or waxed paper, being sure not to disturb topping for 5 minutes. Cut into bars while still warm and then let cool to serve. YIELD: 20 pieces.

RICE KRISPIE SQUARES

¼ c. butter or margarine
4 c. miniature marshmallows
6 c. Rice Krispies

Put marshmallows and margarine in a LARGE bowl. MW FP 2 minutes, stirring twice during cooking time. When finished cooking, stir well again to mix marshmallows. Stir in Rice Krispies. Butter the bottom of a clean glass or cup and use to press mixture into a buttered 9 x 13 inch pan. Let cool. Cut into squares. YIELD: 16 - 20 pieces.

ROCKY ROAD FUDGE POPS

3⅝ oz. pkg. chocolate pudding mix (not instant)
2½ c. milk
½ c. marshmallow creme
⅓ c. chopped peanuts
¼ c. chopped chocolate chips
6 wax coated paper cups (9 oz. size)
6 wooden popsicle sticks

Combine pudding mix and milk in a 4-cup measure. MW FP 5½ - 6 minutes, or until slightly thickened, stirring every 2 minutes. Cool pudding to room temperature. Fold in marshmallow creme to create marbled appearance. Set aside. Mix chopped peanuts and chopped chocolate chips in small bowl. Spoon 1 heaping tablespoon of mixture into each of six cups. Add 1 tablespoon of pudding mixture to each cup and stir lightly to combine. Divide remaining pudding mixture evenly between cups. Insert popsicle stick in center of each cup. Freeze several hours, or until firm. To serve, peel cups from frozen pops.

SCOTCHEROOS

1 c. butterscotch chips
½ c. salted peanuts, coarsely chopped
¼ c. peanut butter
4 c. coarsely crushed corn flake cereal
Maraschino cherries cut into tiny pieces for garnish

In a large bowl combine butterscotch chips and peanut butter. MW PL7 for 1½ - 2 minutes or until melted, stirring every 30 seconds. Add corn flakes and peanuts. Stir until coated. Drop by rounded teaspoons onto waxed paper. Garnish with a piece of cherry if desired. Refrigerate until set. YIELD: not enough.

S'MORE BARS

⅓ c. light corn syrup
1 tbsp. butter or margarine
6 oz. milk chocolate chips
½ tsp. vanilla
4 c. golden grahams cereal
1½ c. miniature marshmallows

Place corn syrup and butter in 3-quart casserole. MW FP 1 - 1½ minutes or until boiling. Stir halfway through cooking.

Add chocolate chips and vanilla. Stir until chocolate is melted. Gradually fold in cereal and marshmallows until completely coated with chocolate. MW FP 15 - 30 seconds or until marshmallows begin to soften. Stir to blend.

Pour into a buttered 9 x 9 x 2 inch pan. Let stand at room temperature for 1 hour. Cut into bars. YIELD: 4 dozen.

SOUTHERN LANE BARS

15 graham cracker squares
3 eggs
1 c. packed brown sugar
½ c. butter or margarine
   melted

½ c. milk
1 c. flaked coconut
1 c. chopped nuts
1 c. graham cracker crumbs
1 tsp. vanilla

*VANILLA ICING:
2 tbsp. butter or margarine
2 c. confectioners' sugar
½ tsp. vanilla

2 - 3 tbsp. milk or
   strong coffee

* Icing may be used to ice or glaze coffee cakes and tube cakes. Prepare half the recipe.

Line bottom of 13 x 9 inch baking dish with graham cracker squares, cutting as necessary to fit. In 2-quart mixing bowl or casserole, combine eggs, sugar, milk and butter; beat well.

MW PL5 for 3 - 6 minutes, or until very thick, stirring every minute. Mixture will not be smooth.

MW FP 2 - 5 minutes, or until mixture is very hot and starts to thicken on sides, stirring every 2 minutes. Stir in remaining ingredients except icing. Spoon over crackers; spread carefully. Cool slightly before frosting.

Put butter in small mixing bowl. MW FP 45 seconds, or until melted. Stir in sugar. Blend in milk gradually, until of spreading consistency. Stir in vanilla. Frost bars. YIELD: 9 x 13 inch pan.

WALNUT BROWNIES

2 oz. unsweetened baking
   chocolate
⅓ c. butter or margarine
1 c. sugar
2 eggs

¾ c. chopped walnuts
1 c. unsifted flour
¼ tsp. baking powder
¼ tsp. salt
½ tsp. vanilla

Put chocolate and butter in large mixing bowl. MW FP 2 minutes or until melted. Stir in sugar. Add eggs. Beat well. Stir in flour, baking powder, salt, vanilla and nuts until moistened.

Spread in greased 8 x 8 inch baking dish. Elevate on rack or inverted bowl. MW FP, uncovered, 5 minutes, or until brownie is puffed and most of top is dry. Cool. Cut into bars. YIELD: 16 - 24 bars.

HINT:

— *Freeze left-over gravy or sauce in ice cube trays for individual servings and reheat as needed in MW.*

EXTRA RECIPES

EXTRA RECIPES

APPLE CRISP

8	apples, peeled and sliced	1	c. brown sugar
2	tsp. cinnamon mixed with	½	c. wheat germ
1	tbsp. white sugar	½	c. chopped nuts
½	c. butter or margarine	1	c. quick cooking oats
1⅓	c. flour	1	c. prepared granola

Mix butter, flour, brown sugar, wheat germ, oats and granola until crumbly. Spread half the mixture into a 9 x 13 inch glass pan. MW FP 2 - 3 minutes or until set. Toss apple slices with cinnamon/sugar mixture in a bowl or casserole. MW FP 4 - 5 minutes or until tender. Spoon over prepared crust. Spoon remaining crumb mixture over top and MW FP 2 minutes, uncovered. Serve warm with ice cream or serve cool with whipped cream or topping. YIELD: 12 - 16 servings.

APPLE CRUMBLE

6	c. (6 med.) peeled, sliced cooking apples	¾	c. brown sugar
1	tbsp. lemon juice	½	c. flour
⅓	c. butter	½	c. rolled oats
		½	tsp. cinnamon or nutmeg

Combine apples and lemon juice in 8-inch square glass baking dish. Set aside. Put butter in glass mixing bowl. MW FP 20 seconds or until softened. Mix in remaining ingredients with fork just until crumbly. Sprinkle over apples. MW FP, uncovered, 12 - 14 minutes or until apples are tender.

For additional browning of topping, place under broiler for a few minutes. YIELD: 6 servings.

CHERRIES JUBILEE

14	oz. can pitted dark cherries, unsweetened	2	tbsp. sugar
1	tbsp. cornstarch	¼	c. Kirsch (cherry brandy) or plain brandy
⅓	c. currant jelly	1½	pts. vanilla ice cream

Drain cherries, reserving juice. Place juice in 1½ - 2 quart glass serving dish. Mix in cornstarch until smooth. Add jelly and sugar. MW FP, uncovered, 2½ minutes or until cherries are heated through. Put Kirsch (cherry brandy) or brandy in glass measure. MW FP 25 seconds. Pour over cherry sauce. Ignite with long match or wooden skewer. Stir until flame subsides. Spoon hot cherries over ice cream. YIELD: 6 servings.

AUNTY PETUNIA'S
LUSCIOUS LEMON SLICE

Now I know what you're thinking . . . who ever heard of an Aunty Petunia? Bear with me while I digress for a moment about unusual names. When I was four years old my older sister came from school telling my Mom, Aunty Petunia and me about a man speaker they had had at school that day . . . Mr. Lee Bumsuck. Well, I laughed, as hard as a four year old could, until tears rolled down my little cheeks. My Mom laughed, my Aunty Petunia laughed and my sister laughed too. Well, when we all ran out of tissue and energy my Mom asked me why I was laughing. So I am told by all who witnessed my ageless wisdom answer . . . "Who ever heard of a man named Lee!?"

Well, that brings me to Aunty Petunia's unusual name. You see Aunty Petunia's real name is actually Gertrude, but every year since we all have known her Aunty Gertie would plant a bed of petunias in her flower garden. One summer after hearing that funny name I gave it to her and it stuck. In terms of unusual names, and no offense is intended - I'd say it's a pretty close race between Petunia and Gertrude!

In any case, Aunty says that everyone has to be good at something, and although she admits that she hates to bake, she takes great pleasure in preparing her luscious lemon slice. It's quick, it's easy and it's her claim to fame - a legacy to her grandchildren and a tribute to the lemon pie filling manufacturers of America - as if her name isn't enough to pass down!!

2	c. water	Whole graham wafer
4	oz. pkg. (approx.) lemon	crackers
	pie filling	Whipped cream or
½	c. granulated sugar	whipped topping
¼	c. cold water	Maraschino cherries
2	egg yolks	

Put 2 cups water in a glass measure. MW FP 4 - 5 minutes or until very hot. Measure ¼ water into a 4-cup measure. Stir in lemon pie filling powder and sugar. Whisk to blend. Whisk in egg yolks. Whisk in 2 cups of heated water.

MW FP 3 - 5 minutes, whisking after every minute to distribute starch and prevent boilovers.

Line a 9 x 13 inch cake pan with whole graham wafers, trimming last few if necessary to fit pan. Pour ⅓ of hot lemon mixture over wafers. Cover with second layer of graham wafers. Pour ⅓ of hot lemon mixture over wafers. Place third layer of graham wafers over lemon filling and pour last ⅓ of lemon mixture over last layer of graham wafers. Cover with plastic wrap and chill.

Garnish with whipped cream or whipped topping and maraschino cherries. YIELD: 12 - 16 servings.

BLACK FOREST TRIFLE

19 oz. pkg. (2 layer size) chocolate cake mix*	2½ c. milk
½ c. Kirsch or cherry brandy	2 egg yolks, beaten
22 oz. can cherry pie filling	1 c. whipping cream
4 oz. pkg. chocolate pudding & pie filling mix (not instant)	2 tbsp. icing sugar
	Chocolate curls
	Maraschino cherries with stems

*Bake cake mix, according to instructions on page 80 (Triple Chocolate Bundt Cake).

Place one cake layer in bottom of trifle bowl or other deep serving dish. Sprinkle with ¼ cup Kirsch or cherry brandy. Spread cherry pie filling on top. Place second cake layer on pie filling. Sprinkle with rest of Kirsch or cherry brandy.

Place pudding mix in 1½-quart casserole. Add milk gradually, stirring to blend well. MW FP 6 - 8 minutes, stirring every 3 minutes, until thickened. Gradually stir half pudding into beaten yolks. Return egg mixture to casserole, stirring well. MW PL7 for 4 - 6 minutes, stirring every 2 minutes, until thickened. Cool.

Pour cooled pudding over cake in dish. Whip cream with icing sugar. Spread over pudding. Garnish with chocolate curls and maraschino cherries. Chill 4 hours or more, before serving. YIELD: 8 - 10 servings.

PEACH CRUMBLE

1 c. flour	¼ tsp. nutmeg
½ c. brown sugar	1 tsp. grated lemon peel
½ c. crushed corn flakes or other dry cereal flakes	1 tsp. lemon juice
½ tsp. soda	½ c. butter or margarine, softened
½ tsp. salt	2 - 14 oz. cans peach slices, drained
½ tsp. cinnamon	

In large bowl, combine all ingredients, except peaches. Mix until crumbly and well blended.

Press half mixture into bottom of greased glass 9-inch square dish. Arrange peach slices over mixture. Sprinkle on remaining crumb mixture.

MW FP 7 minutes in microwave oven. Serve warm or cold with whipped cream. YIELD: 6 servings.

HINT:

— Fresh parsley will chop easily if microwaved a few seconds.

BOBBALOUIE'S TERRIFIC TRIFLE

Just like Aunty Petunia says, everyone has to be good at something. Well, Bobbalouie does a great number of things very well, and although she won't always be remembered for all of them, there are three things I'll never forget about her:

How much she hates her nickname (funny names seem to run in the family); how much everyone likes her terrific trifle, and the fact that she has always been and always will be my very best friend in the whole world - she's my Mom!

2 - 6 oz. pkgs. vanilla pudding and pie filling (not instant)	Bananas, cut in coins
	Fresh strawberries
2½ c. milk (approx.), ½ cup less than called for on each pkg.	Canned peach slices, well drained
	Any other canned fruit slices, well drained, or
1 lge. or several individual jelly roll cakes	Suitable fresh fruit in season
Brandy*	Whipped cream

* Use cherry brandy, banana liqueur, peach brandy, sweet sherry or other sweet liqueur or fruit juice if you wish the trifle to contain no alcohol.

Whisk milk together with pudding mixes in a very large micro-proof bowl. MW FP 5 minutes, until milk is very hot, whisking after 3 minutes and at the end of the 5 minutes. MW PL7 until mixture boils, whisking every 2 minutes. Allow to cool for 5 minutes.

Slice jelly roll into ½-inch vertical slices and lay on bottom of trifle bowl. Cut a few of the vertical slices horizontally - you will have half circles. Stand the flat edge on the bottom layer of cake, pressing the half circles against the side of the bowl. The jelly roll will show through the bowl displaying an attractive scallop of cake.

Generously sprinkle with liqueur or fruit juice to moisten. Place a layer of fruit over the moistened cake. You may wish to mix the fruit in each layer or you can use one different type of fruit per layer. Cover fruit with a layer of pudding so that it is just covered.

Continue layering fruit and pudding until you have just enough space left for whipped cream.

Cover with plastic wrap and chill. When trifle is cold, garnish with whipped cream and attractively arranged fruit on top. When serving use a long handled spoon, being sure to serve some of the cake with each portion.

PUMPKIN PIE SQUARES

¾ c. flour
¾ c. quick cooking oats
½ c. chopped walnuts
½ c. butter, softened
4 oz. pkg. butterscotch
   pudding & pie filling mix
   (not instant)

1 c. flaked or shredded
   coconut
1½ tsp. pumpkin pie spice
16 oz. can pumpkin
15 oz. can sweetened
   condensed milk
2 eggs

In large mixing bowl, combine flour, oats, nuts, butter and dry pudding mix. Mix until crumbly. Press into bottom and sides of ungreased 12 x 8 x 2 inch glass baking dish.

In same mixing bowl, combine coconut, pumpkin, pumpkin pie spice, milk and eggs. Blend well. Pour over crust in dish.

Place dish in microwave oven. MW FP 14 - 16 minutes, giving dish a quarter turn every 5 minutes. When done, knife inserted into custard in centre comes our clean. YIELD: 12 - 15 squares.

HINT:
— *To toast coconut MW FP 2 - 3 minutes, stirring after each minute.*

RASPBERRY STREUSEL BARS

¾ c. butter
1 c. light brown sugar,
   packed
1½ c. unsifted all-purpose flour
1 tsp. baking powder

½ tsp. salt
1½ c. quick-cooking oatmeal
1 c. finely chopped pecans
1 sm. jar raspberry jam

Place butter in an 8-inch square dish. MW FP 1 - 2 minutes, until melted.

Stir in brown sugar, flour, baking powder, salt, oatmeal and pecans, stirring to blend well.

Remove about half of crumbs and set aside.

Press remaining crumbs evenly over bottom of dish to form base. Spread base with jam, then sprinkle with remaining crumbs.

MW FP 7 - 10 minutes, rotating dish quarter turn after 4 minutes. When done, bars will be soft but appear set at edges. Top layer will look dry.

Cool completely, then cut into bars. YIELD: 30 bars.

HINT:
— *To scald one cup of milk MW FP 2 - 2½ minutes.*

EXTRA RECIPES

EXTRA RECIPES

APPLE JAM

2	med. apples. cored & peeled	1½ c. sugar	
		1 tsp. lemon juice	

Combine apples and sugar in medium bowl. MW FP until apples are tender, 3 - 5 minutes. Beat softened apple mixture with electric mixer until well blended. MW FP until mixture is slightly thickened, 3 - 4 minutes, stirring once during cooking time. Stir in lemon juice. Pour into prepared jars, seal, and refrigerate. YIELD: 1 - 1½ cups.

APPLE SAUCE

4	c. sliced peeled tart apples	¼ - ½ c. sugar	
½	c. water	¼ tsp. ground cinnamon	

Place all ingredients in 1-quart casserole; cover. MW FP until apples are tender, 7 - 10 minutes. Mash apples to desired consistency. Serve warm or chilled. YIELD: 4 - 6 servings.

VARIATION:

Add 3 tablespoons red cinnamon candies to applesauce. MW FP 30 seconds to 1 minute 30 seconds. Stir until candies are dissolved.

BAKES APPLES WITH CARAMEL SAUCE

4	cooking apples, cored & cut in half lengthwise	⅓ - ½ c. milk	
25	vanilla caramels	¼ c. chopped nuts	

Place apples, cut side up, in an 8 x 8 x 2 inch baking dish. Cover with a tight fitting lid or plastic wrap. MW FP 3 - 4 minutes or until apples are just tender. Combine caramels and milk in a 2-cup measure. MW FP 2 - 3 minutes or until melted. Stir halfway through cooking. Pour caramel sauce over apples and sprinkle with nuts. MW uncovered FP 2 - 3 minutes or until sauce is bubbly and apples are tender. Serve warm. YIELD: 4 servings.

CINNAMON BAKED APPLES

4	lge. baking apples (2½ - 3 inch diameter)	4 tbsp. red cinnamon candies	

Core apples without cutting through bottom skin and peel about 1-inch strip of skin from stem end of each apple. If necessary, cut thin slice from bottom of each apple so it will stand upright.

Arrange apples in shallow baking dish. Place 1 tablespoon of the cinnamon candies in center of each apple. MW FP until apples are tender, 4 - 6 minutes. Rearrange apples once. YIELD: 4 servings.

FRUIT-FILLED PINEAPPLE BOATS

1	med. sized fresh pineapple	½	c. maraschino cherries
½	c. toasted sliced almonds		without stems, drained
10	oz. can mandarin orange	½	c. sweet orange marmalade
	sections, drained		mixed with
½	c. seedless grapes	2	tbsp. lemon juice
1	banana, sliced	¼	c. light rum

Cut pineapple, including leafy crown, in half lengthwise. Cut out fruit, leaving outside shell intact. Remove woody core. Cut remaining fruit in chunks. Toss pineapple chunks with almonds, oranges, grapes, banana, cherries and marmalade/lemon juice mixture. Place pineapple shells in 13 x 9 x 2 inch dish or on serving plate suitable for microwave oven. Fill shells with fruit mixture. Cover with waxed paper. MW FP 10 minutes. Pour rum into glass measuring cup. MW FP 30 seconds. Remove one metal tablespoonful. Pour rest of rum over pineapple. Ignite rum in spoon. Pour over pineapple to flame. YIELD: 6 servings.

EASY PINEAPPLE PRESERVES

8	oz. can crushed pineapple,	2	tbsp. honey
	in its own juice, undrained	1	tsp. grated orange peel
1	tbsp. cornstarch		

Mix all ingredients in deep 1-quart bowl. MW FP until thickened, 2 - 4 minutes, stirring after half the cooking time. Pour into prepared jars, seal and refrigerate. YIELD: ¾ cup.

FRUIT KEBABS

1½	tsp. cornstarch	4	oz. pineapple chunks,
⅛	tsp. cinnamon		drained
2	tbsp. lemon juice	4	oz. mandarin oranges,
2	tbsp. orange juice		drained
1½	tbsp. honey	1	sm. banana, cut into
1	sm. apple, cut into		½-inch slices
	1-inch cubes	6	skewers

In measuring cup mix cornstarch, cinnamon, lemon juice, orange juice and honey. MW FP 1 - 2 minutes, or until thick, stirring once or twice.

Alternate apple, pineapple, orange and banana on skewers to fill each skewer. Brush with glaze.

Refrigerate. Brush with hot glaze again before serving. YIELD: 6 servings.

FRUIT JELLY

6   oz. can frozen apple,   1¾ oz. pkg. powdered
    grape, pineapple or   fruit pectin
    tangerine juice concentrate 3½ c. sugar
2   c. water

In 3-quart casserole or 8-cup measure combine juice concentrate and water. Stir in pectin until dissolved. MW FP 7 - 14 minutes, or until boiling, stirring every 3 minutes. Boil 1 minute. Gradually stir in sugar until blended.

MW FP 5 - 7 minutes, or until mixture returns to a boil, stirring carefully every 2 minutes, to prevent boilover. Boil 1 minute. Skim any foam from top. Pour into hot sterilized ½ pint jars. Cover with hot sterilized lids and screw bands. Invert jar and quickly return to upright position. Or, if desired, seal jars with paraffin wax. Store in a cool, dark place no longer than 6 months. YIELD: 2½ pints.

VARIATIONS:

ZESTY GRAPE JELLY — Stir 1 teaspoon fresh lemon juice into grape jelly after skimming foam.

MINT APPLE JELLY — Stir 5 - 7 drops green food coloring & 1 teaspoon mint extract into apple jelly after skimming foam.

KNOCK KNOCK: Who's there?. . .Banana!. . .Banana who?
KNOCK KNOCK: Who's there?. . .Banana!. . .Banana who?
KNOCK KNOCK: Who's there?. . .Orange!. . .Orange who?
           Orange ya glad I didn't say banana again?!

With thanks to Kyle's "Sick Riddle of the Day" Club, we'll get on to the next recipe!

ORANGE MARMALADE

2   med. oranges   3   tbsp. (½ box) Certo
2   med. lemons   crystals
1¼ c. water   2   c. sugar
⅛   tsp. baking soda

Remove zest from orange and lemon carefully, on grater, being sure not to get pith layer into shavings. Put rinds, water and baking soda into an 8-cup casserole.

Cover, MW FP 2 minutes and then MW PL2 for 8 minutes, stirring twice during cooking. Remove pith layer from fruit and chop pulp of fruit finely.

Add to rind mixture. Simmer, covered, FP 1 minute and PL2 for five minutes. Add Certo. MW FP 7 minutes. Stir in sugar. MW FP 6 minutes, boiling hard for 1 minute. Skim and stir for 7 minutes.

Pour into sterile jars and seal. YIELD: 2 cups.

PEACH CHUTNEY

2 - 16 oz. cans peaches,
    undrained & chopped
1   tart cooking apple, peeled,
    cored & chopped
1   c. chopped celery
¾   c. cider vinegar
½   c. sugar
½   c. currants or raisins
1   tbsp. candied lemon peel
½   tsp. salt
¼   tsp. cinnamon
¼   tsp. ginger

Mix all ingredients in a 3-quart casserole. Cover loosely with lid or plastic wrap. MW FP 15 - 16 minutes or until boiling. Uncover. MW PL5 for 45 - 50 minutes or until syrup is thickened. Stir occasionally during cooking. Pour into hot sterilized jars. Cover tightly. Store in refrigerator. Serve with meats. YIELD: four 8 oz. jars.

RASPBERRY JAM

2 - 10 oz. pkg. frozen
    raspberries
2½ c. sugar
1   tbsp. lemon juice
3   tbsp. plus 1½ tsp. liquid
    pectin

Place frozen raspberries in 2-quart casserole. MW FP until thawed, 4 - 6 minutes. Stir in sugar and lemon juice. MW FP until mixture boils, 8 - 10 minutes, stirring after half the cooking time. Blend in liquid pectin.

MW FP until mixture comes to a rolling boil, 3 - 4 minutes. MW FP to continue boiling, 1 minute. Pour into prepared jars, seal and refrigerate. YIELD: 2½ - 3 cups.

RHUBARB FRUIT LEATHER

Wash and cut rhubarb into ½-inch pieces. Put 4 cups rhubarb and ½ cup water in casserole. MW FP 5 - 7 minutes or until rhubarb starts to soften. Cool slightly. Put in blender or food processor and puree. Combine 2 cups puree with 3 tablespoons honey (or more to taste).

Lay a sheet of plastic wrap on a microproof plate or tray. Pour puree to ¼-inch thick, spreading mixture by tilting the dish, do not use a spatula or knife. MW PL5 for 20 minutes. Let stand 5 minutes. The leather will be sticky to the touch, but will peel off the plastic wrap. Lift the edge of the plastic wrap and peel it back about 1 inch. If it peels easily, it is ready, if not MW PL5 for 2 - 3 minutes at a time, allowing to stand 5 minutes between cooking. To store the fruit leather, roll with plastic backing loosely and store indefinitely in the freezer, months in the refrigerator or up to 6 months at 70° F. Simply cut off as much as you like with scissors.

RHUBARB/STRAWBERRY FRUIT LEATHER

Make rhubarb puree as for Rhubarb Fruit Leather. Using fresh, or frozen strawberries, puree to get 1 cup of strawberry puree. Combine 1 cup rhubarb and 1 cup strawberry puree. Add 1½ tbsp. honey (or more to taste). Dry as for rhubarb fruit leather.

STRAWBERRY JAM

Ah, Strawberries, so sweet, so juicy, so delicious, so few calories. The perfect food. How did Mother Nature ever come up with that combination, seems too good to be true. Ummm, just taste one bite . . . oops! Dropped it on the white dining room rug - hmmm, quite a stain!

Knew it was too good to be true, it's not perfect after all. Oh well, as one strawberry said to the other, if you hadn't been so fresh we wouldn't have got into this jam!

2	pts. strawberries, washed, hulled & crushed or	3	tbsp. or ½ box Certo crystals
2	c. thawed & crushed, frozen strawberries,	3	c. sugar

Combine strawberries and Certo in a 1½-quart casserole. MW FP 5 - 6 minutes, or until jam comes to a boil, stirring once. Add sugar and mix well. MW FP 4 - 5 minutes or until jam has boiled hard for 1 minute, stirring once.

Remove from microwave oven, stir and skim foam. Let cool slightly for 5 minutes to prevent fruit from floating to the tops of the jars. Ladle into sterile glass jars and seal. YIELD: 6 small jars.

STUFFED APPLES

4	apples	2	tsp. cinnamon
¼	c. brown sugar	2	tbsp. butter
¼	c. slivered almonds		Sweet or sour cream
¼	c. raisins		

Wash and core apples. Place in 8 x 8 inch glass baking dish. Place brown sugar and butter in centre of each apple. Add raisins and slivered almonds. Sprinkle with cinnamon.

MW FP 5 minutes or until tender. Serve warm with sweet or sour cream. YIELD: 4 servings.

STRAWBERRIES 'N' CREME

¼ c. sugar
2 tsp. cornstarch
Dash salt
1½ c. milk
2 eggs, separated
½ tsp. vanilla
¼ c. sugar

1 pt. strawberries,
rinsed & hulled or
16 oz. pkg. whole,
unsweetened strawberries,
thawed & drained
½ tsp. vanilla

Blend ¼ cup sugar, cornstarch and salt in 1-quart casserole. Stir in milk. Blend in egg yolks.

MW PL7 until mixture coats a metal spoon, 2½ - 5 minutes, blending with wire whisk once or twice. Chill. Stir in ½ teaspoon vanilla.

Just before serving, divide strawberries among 4 small bowls. Beat egg whites until foamy. Beat in ¼ cup sugar, 1 tablespoon at a time; continue beating until stiff peaks form. Beat in ½ teaspoon vanilla.

Pour custard sauce over strawberries. Top each with meringue. MW PL7 until meringues are set, 45 seconds to 1 minute 15 seconds. Rearrange once during cooking. YIELD: 4 servings.

PIE CRUST - HOW TO MICROWAVE

Form dough into 6-inch flattened patty. Refrigerate 30 minutes. Roll out to 9-inch circle. Fit into plate. Flute edge. Prick all over with tines of fork.

Cover with waxed paper and weight with dry lentils, or fit second pie plate over top of waxed paper.

MW PL7 for 6 - 8 minutes or until pastry appears dry and opaque, turning every 2 minutes.

CHERRY LEMON TARTS

24	cupcake liners	14	oz. can sweetened
2	tbsp. butter or margarine		condensed milk
1	c. graham cracker crumbs	1	tbsp. grated lemon peel
2	tbsp. sugar	1/3	c. lemon juice
2	eggs	21	oz. can cherry pie filling

Place 2 liners in each 5 or 6 oz. custard cup. Put butter in small bowl. MW FP 45 seconds or until melted. Stir in crumbs and sugar. Place 1 rounded tablespoon crumb mixture in each liner. Press down firmly with small glass. Blend remaining ingredients except pie filling until thickened. Place 2 tablespoons in each cup. Arrange 6 cups in ring in oven.

MW PL5 for 2 - 5 minutes, or just until each bubbles in 1 or 2 spots, rotating after half the time. Remove tarts as they appear done. Cool and serve topped with pie filling. YIELD: 12 servings.

NOTE: If less than 6 are microwaved at a time allow 20 - 30 seconds per cup.

EASY LEMON FREEZE

2	tbsp. butter or margarine	1/2	c. Realemon reconstituted
1	c. graham cracker crumbs		lemon juice
21	oz. can lemon pie filling	1½	c. whipped topping
1	can Eagle Brand sweetened condensed milk		Lemon slices (optional)

Put butter in 8 x 8 inch microproof dish. MW FP 30 seconds or until melted. Stir in crumbs. Press evenly onto bottom of dish to form crust. MW FP 2 minutes, rotating dish ½ turn after 1 minute. Cool.

In medium bowl, combine pie filling, sweetened condensed milk and lemon juice. Mix until smooth. Spread into prepared pan. Top with whipped topping and reserved crumbs. Freeze 3 hours. If desired, garnish with lemon slices before serving. YIELD: 9 servings.

CHOCOLATE ALMOND MOUSSE PIE

Mousse, Moose or Mousse - no matter how you spell it, it spells t-r-o-u-b-l-e! A lot of calories, a lot of haircare or a lot of bull! Lord knows we spend too much energy on our hair and get far too much bull served up every day, so let's get down to business and talk about some real calories, my favorite, chocolate mousse.

¼ c. margarine or butter	4 oz. pkg. chocolate
1¼ c. fine chocolate wafer	pudding & pie filling
cookie crumbs	(not instant)
½ tsp. almond extract	¾ c. chilled whipping cream
1½ c. milk	¼ c. toasted sliced almonds

Place margarine in 9-inch pie plate. MW FP until melted, 30 seconds to 1 minute 15 seconds. Add chocolate cookie crumbs; mix thoroughly. Press mixture firmly against bottom and side of pie plate.

MW PL7 until hot, 2½ - 4½ minutes. Rotate pie plate once or twice during cooking. Cool completely before filling.

Blend pudding mix and milk in 1½-quart casserole. MW FP until thick and bubbly, 4 - 7 minutes, stirring once or twice. Place plastic wrap directly on surface of pudding. Refrigerate until cool but not set, stirring with wire whisk several times.

When pudding is cool but not set, stir in almond extract. Beat whipping cream in chilled bowl until stiff. Fold pudding into whipped cream. Spoon into crust. Refrigerate until set, 2 - 4 hours. Sprinkle with toasted almonds. YIELD: 9-inch pie.

CREME DE MENTHE ICE CREAM PIE

5 tbsp. melted margarine	¼ c. Creme de Menthe
2 tbsp. sugar	2 - 3 drops green food
1⅓ c. graham cracker crumbs	coloring
1 qt. vanilla ice cream	

Combine melted margarine, sugar and graham crumbs. Press into 9-inch pie plate. MW FP 1½ minutes. Place ice cream in mixer bowl and slice into 4 pieces. MW PL5 for 45 - 60 seconds until slightly soft, NOT melted. Beat in flavoring with electric beater at low speed.

Freeze 2 hours before serving. Let your imagination create new flavours. YIELD: 6 servings.

CRUMBLE CRUST APPLE PIE

CRUMBLE PASTRY:

2 c. flour	⅓ c. cold water
1 tsp. salt	6 - 7 drops yellow food
⅔ c. shortening	coloring
3 tbsp. margarine	

APPLE FILLING:

4 - 5 c. sliced, pared apples	1 tsp. cinnamon
⅔ c. sugar	2 tbsp. flour

In large mixing bowl combine flour, salt, shortening and margarine. Mix on lowest speed of mixer or with pastry blender until particles resemble coarse crumbs.

Remove 1½ cups mixture to pie plate. Combine water and food coloring. Sprinkle 2 tablespoons over crumbs in plate, tossing with fork until well mixed but crumbly. Spread over bottom of plate. MW FP 4 - 6 minutes. Cool and crumble finely. Set aside.

Sprinkle remaining water over mixture in bowl, while stirring with fork, just until moist. Roll out with rolling pin; fit into pie plate; pierce with tines of fork; and weight down using wax paper and dried legumes or rice. MW FP 5 - 7 minutes, rotating dish ½ turn every 3 minutes. If crust is cooking unevenly, rotate ¼ turn every minute. Crust will appear dry and opaque when done.

Prepare apples as directed below. Spread filling in cooked shell. Sprinkle with reserved crumbs. MW FP 14 - 18 minutes, or until apples are tender, rotating ¼ turn after 6 minutes, then every 3 - 4 minutes.

Place apples evenly in cooked pastry shell. Sprinkle with sugar, flour, and cinnamon. Sprinkle on crumble topping (above) and bake.

NOTE: Microwave pies bubble hard. Place waxed paper in oven to catch spills. Power Level may be reduced to Medium-High (PL7) or Medium (PL5); add more time if needed.

DOUBLE CRUSTED FRUIT PIE

Roll out pie crust. Line pie plate. Fill with fruit. Put on top crust, seal with fluted edges. Cut slits in top. Preheat conventional oven to 450° F. While conventional oven is preheating, brush pie with milk and sprinkle lightly with sugar and then MW FP 7 - 8 minutes. Transfer to heated conventional oven and cook 10 - 15 minutes or until crust is golden brown.

DEEP DISH APPLE PIE

1 tbsp. sugar	2 tbsp. all-purpose flour
½ tsp. ground cinnamon	¾ c. buttermilk biscuit baking
5 c. sliced peeled apples	mix or basic biscuit mix
½ c. sugar	⅓ c. milk
½ tsp. ground cinnamon	2 tbsp. sugar
or cloves	

Mix 1 tablespoon sugar and ½ teaspoon cinnamon; set aside. Combine apples, ½ cup sugar, flour and ½ teaspoon cinnamon or cloves in 1-quart casserole. Cover. MW FP until apples are tender and sauce is bubbly, 3 - 4 minutes.

Mix buttermilk biscuit baking mix, milk and 2 tablespoons sugar just until moistened. Drop by spoonfuls onto hot apple mixture. Sprinkle with cinnamon-sugar mixture. MW FP until topping is set, 4 - 6 minutes. Serve with whipped cream, if desired. YIELD: 4 - 6 servings.

FRUIT FLAN

CRUST:

⅔ c. butter or margarine	⅓ c. sifted icing sugar
1¼ c. flour	Dash cinnamon

FILLING:

	GLAZE:
1 apple, pared & sliced	⅓ c. orange juice
¼ c. orange juice	¼ c. black currant or
14 oz. can apricot halves,	raspberry jam
drained	1 tsp. sugar
1 banana, sliced	1 tsp. cornstarch
½ c. blueberries or	Dash nutmeg
3 strawberries, halved	1 tsp. gelatin

Prepare crust by creaming butter or margarine with icing sugar. Stir in flour and cinnamon to make a soft dough. Roll out ¼-inch thick and place in a lightly greased 9-inch glass pie plate or glass flan dish. Prick sides and bottom with fork.

Cover with waxed paper, elevate and MW FP 4 - 5 minutes. Rotate dish as necessary, until cooked. Set aside to cool. Put apple slices in orange juice and MW FP 20 - 40 seconds until tender. Arrange fruit attractively in baked crust.

Prepare glaze by combining all glaze ingredients, except gelatin, in a 2-cup glass measure. MW FP, uncovered, 2 - 3 minutes until mixture boils and thickens slightly. Stir in gelatin until completely dissolved. Let cool and spoon evenly over fruit. Chill well before serving. Top with whipped cream if desired. YIELD: 6 servings.

GRASSHOPPER PIE

¼ c. butter	2 tbsp. white Creme de Cacao
1¼ c. fine chocolate cookie crumbs	1 c. whipping cream, whipped
2 tbsp. sugar	Chocolate curls or
10 oz. pkg. lge. marshmallows	reserved crumb mixture
½ c. milk	Whipped cream
¼ c. Creme de Menthe	

Place butter in 9-inch pie plate. MW FP 30 seconds, until melted. Blend in crumbs and sugar. If desired, reserve 2 tablespoons crumb mixture for garnish. Press crust firmly and evenly into pie plate. MW FP 2 - 2½ minutes, rotating dish half turn after 1 minute. Cool.

Place marshmallows and milk into 3-quart casserole. Cover. MW FP 2 - 3 minutes, until mixture can be stirred smooth. Chill in refrigerator 30 - 40 minutes or until thickened, stirring occasionally.

Stir in Creme de Menthe and Creme de Cacao. Fold in whipped cream. Pour into crust. Decorate with chocolate curls or reserved crumbs and additional whipped cream, if desired. Refrigerate several hours or overnight. YIELD: 9-inch pie.

LEMON MERINGUE PIE

CRUST:	MERINGUE:
¼ c. butter	2 egg whites
1¼ c. graham wafer crumbs	½ tsp. cream of tartar
¼ c. sugar	4 tbsp. sugar

CRUST: Put butter in pie plate. MW FP 1 minute or until melted. Blend crumbs and sugar and mix with butter in pie plate. Press into plate. MW FP 2 - 2½ minutes. Cool.

FILLING: Use packaged lemon pie filling. Prepare as per package instructions but use a glass bowl instead of a saucepan. Combine ingredients. MW FP 3 minutes. Whisk. MW FP 3 minutes. Pour into cooled pie crust.

MERINGUE: Beat egg whites with cream of tartar until stiff peaks are formed. Gradually add sugar and beat until it is dissolved and no graininess remains in the meringue. Spread on cooled pie. MW PL7 for 3 - 4 minutes to set meringue. YIELD: 6 - 8 servings.

HINT:

— *To blanch vegetables MW FP 3 minutes/pound.*

NEVER FAIL PASTRY

5	c. all-purpose flour	1	lb. vegetable shortening
4	tsp. brown sugar	1	egg
½	tsp. baking powder	1	tbsp. vinegar
½	tsp. salt	¾	c. milk

Combine first 4 ingredients. Cut in shortening until mixture resembles small peas. Break egg into a 1 cup measure. Beat with a fork. Add vinegar and add enough milk to measure 1 cup. Mix and pour into flour mixture, stirring with a fork until well blended. Form into a ball, cover and chill. Divide into 5 portions. Freezes well. Roll out pastry large enough to line pie plate. Brush edges with a mixture of 1 tablespoon brown sugar mixed with 1 tablespoon water. Prick with tines of a fork. MW FP 3 minutes. Rotate ¼ turn and MW FP 2 - 3 minutes. Cool and fill. YIELD: 5 single crusts.

HINT:

— *Barbecue steaks or hamburgers to very rare. Let cool, wrap and freeze. Defrost and finish cooking in MW.*

PUDDINGS AND CUSTARDS - HOW TO MICROWAVE

The microwave is great for puddings and custards. You do not need a double boiler and do not have to constantly stir the mixture. Further, if you follow instructions, the chances of scorching the mixture are slim. I prefer to cook pudding and custard mixtures in a glass measuring cup, as it is easy to handle and it is already in use for measuring.

Unless otherwise instructed in particular recipes, microwave puddings at full power and custards at fifty percent power (PL5).

Measure liquid in measuring cup, add balance of ingredients, whisk, cook two minutes, whisk again. The whisking is very important as it distributes the starch and makes for a smooth final product. Continue to cook until pudding or custard thickens or boils.

The time needed to cook a double crust pie can be reduced dramatically by using the microwave in conjunction with your conventional oven.

Preheat conventional oven to 450° F. Prepare pie, seal edges, cut slits in top crust. Brush top crust and edges with milk and sprinkle lightly with granulated sugar, MW FP 7 - 8 minutes. Transfer to preheated oven and bake at 450° F. for 10 - 15 minutes.

BAKED CUSTARD

1¾ c. milk	¼ tsp. salt
¼ c. sugar	½ tsp. vanilla
3 eggs	Nutmeg

Combine all ingredients, except nutmeg, in a 4-cup measuring cup. Beat well with rotary beater. Pour into four 6 oz. glass custard cups, ¾ full. Sprinkle nutmeg on top of each. MW PL3 for 15 - 16 minutes or until knife comes out clean when inserted near centre of each. Let stand 5 minutes before serving.

NOTE: Custards cook at slightly different rates, therefore remove custards from oven as they finish cooking.

HOT FUDGE PUDDING

1 c. flour	2 tbsp. vegetable oil
2 tsp. baking powder	1 tsp. vanilla
½ tsp. salt	1¼ c. boiling water
½ c. sugar	TOPPING:
2 tbsp. cocoa	3 tbsp. cocoa
½ c. milk	½ c. sugar

Mix dry ingredients. Put liquid ingredients into a 2-quart casserole. Add dry ingredients and stir until just blended. Mix topping ingredients. Sprinkle topping over pudding. Pour boiling water over entire pudding. MW PL7 for 9 minutes, uncovered.

CREME VANILLA
WITH BLUBERRY TOPPING

½	c. water	¾	c. dairy sour cream
1	env. unflavored gelatin	2	c. frozen blueberries
¾	c. sugar	¾	tsp. lemon juice
1	c. light cream	⅓	c. sugar
½	tsp. vanilla	2	tsp. cornstarch
¼	tsp. salt		

Put water in glass measure. MW FP until boiling, 45 seconds to 1 minute 15 seconds. Stir in gelatin until dissolved. Combine gelatin mixture and ¾ cup sugar in medium bowl; stir to dissolve sugar.

Stir in cream, vanilla and salt. Chill until mixture begins to set. Beat with electric mixer until smooth. Beat in sour cream. Spoon into 4 lightly oiled individual dishes. Chill at least 4 hours.

Put blueberries in microproof colander and place over bowl. MW PL7 until completely thawed, 4 - 5½ minutes. Let stand 5 minutes. Reserve juice. Mash ⅓ cup of the blueberries in small bowl. Add reserved juice and lemon juice. Blend in ⅓ cup sugar and the cornstarch. MW FP until thick and bubbly, 45 seconds to 1 minute 30 seconds. Let stand until cool. Stir in remaining blueberries. Unmold vanilla cream onto dessert plates. Top each with one-fourth of the blueberry mixture. YIELD: 4 servings.

MINUTE TAPIOCA PUDDING

3	tbsp. minute tapioca*	1	egg yolk
3	tbsp. sugar	½	tsp. vanilla
⅛	tsp. salt	1	egg white
2	c. milk	2	tbsp. sugar

Mix together tapioca, sugar, salt, milk and egg yolk in a 1½-quart glass casserole dish. Let stand 5 minutes. MW FP 3 minutes, uncovered. Stir. MW FP 3½ minutes or until mixture comes to full boil. Stir in vanilla. Allow mixture to stand at room temperature. Beat egg white until foamy. Slowly beat in 2 tablespoons sugar. Whip to soft peaks. Fold into hot mixture. Let stand 10 minutes before serving, covered. This dessert can be served warm or chilled.

* If serving this dessert warm, use 3½ tablespoons minute tapioca instead of 3 tablespoons. YIELD: approx. 6 servings.

QUICK RICE PUDDING

3½ oz. pkg. vanilla pudding		½	c. quick cooking rice
(not instant)		½	c. raisins
2	c. whole milk	¼	tsp. cinnamon

In a 2-quart casserole blend pudding mix, milk and rice. MW FP 6 - 8 minutes, stirring once or twice, until boiling. Add raisins and cinnamon. Cover, let stand 5 - 10 minutes. Stir. Chill. YIELD: 5 - 6 servings.

STEAMED CHRISTMAS PUDDING

4 c. all-purpose flour	2¼ c. chopped walnuts
1½ c. sugar	4 eggs
1 c. dry bread crumbs	1 c. orange juice
1 tsp. cinnamon	1 c. apple juice
½ tsp. ground cloves	¾ c. brandy
½ tsp. nutmeg	2 c. finely grated carrots
2½ c. raisins	1 c. molasses
1 c. diced candied cherries	1 tsp. baking soda
1 c. mixed peel	

Stir together in a large mixing bowl the flour, sugar, bread crumbs and spices.

Stir in raisins, candied cherries, peel and nuts until evenly coated with flour mixture.

In a separate bowl beat eggs. Blend in juices and brandy. Stir in grated carrots. Add liquid mixture to dry ingredients and mix well. Cover and refrigerate, or store in a cool place overnight.

Next day, stir baking soda into molasses. Add to pudding mixture; stir and fold until molasses is blended through.

Makes approximately 11 cups of batter.

Lightly grease a 4-cup microwave-safe measuring cup. Fill with pudding batter to 2⅔ cup level. Cover tightly with a sheet of pleated plastic wrap and MW FP 8 - 10 minutes. Let cool, covered, 10 minutes. Run a knife around edge of cup; invert onto serving plate.

Repeat with remaining batter until all is used.

NOTE: When done, pudding surface will look dry, but sides have not yet pulled away from edge of measuring cup.

For individual puddings: lightly grease microwave-safe muffin pans or custard cups. Fill each cup with 2 - 3 tablespoons of batter. Cover tightly with pleated plastic wrap. MW FP 3 - 5 minutes. Let cool, covered, 10 minutes.

To store, sprinkle cooled pudding with 2 or 3 tablespoons brandy. Wrap tightly in plastic wrap and store in refrigerator up to one month.

To serve large pudding: leaving pudding wrapped in plastic wrap, MW FP 2 - 4 minutes. Unwrap and place on serving plate. Serve with sauce spooned over top.

For a special effect, warm ¼ cup brandy in a glass measuring cup. MW FP 30 seconds; pour over pudding and ignite.

STEAMED CHRISTMAS PUDDING SAUCE

2	tbsp. butter	1	tsp. brandy extract or
1	tbsp. all-purpose flour	1	tsp. rum extract or
¼	c. sugar	2	tbsp. rum or
	Few grains salt	2	tbsp. brandy
1	c. boiling water		Few grains nutmeg
1	tsp. vanilla or		

Put butter in a microproof 2-cup measure. MW FP 30 seconds or until melted. Whisk in flour. Whisk in sugar and salt. Whisk constantly while adding boiling water. MW FP 1 - 3 minutes or until mixture is clear and thickened, whisking once or twice during cooking. Add flavoring and nutmeg. YIELD: 1 cup.

STEAMED CRANBERRY PUDDING

1	c. fresh or frozen cranberries	2	eggs
		1	c. all-purpose flour
½	c. golden raisins	½	c. fine soft bread crumbs
2	tsp. grated orange peel	1	tsp. baking powder
2	tbsp. strong hot tea	½	tsp. baking soda
2	tbsp. honey	¼	tsp. salt
½	c. butter	¼	tsp. nutmeg
½	c. sugar		

Coarsely chop cranberries in food processor, or halve by hand. Combine with raisins and orange peel. Stir in hot tea and honey; set aside.

In a large bowl, cream butter and sugar together until light. Beat in eggs one at a time.

Combine dry ingredients and add to butter-egg mixture, mixing well. Stir in cranberry mixture.

Pour batter into a well-buttered 6-cup microwave-safe ring mold. Cover with plastic wrap, MW PL7 for 8 - 10 minutes, or until a toothpick inserted in the centre comes out clean. Let stand covered 10 minutes, then unmold.

To reheat: Cover with plastic wrap. MW PL5 for 4 - 6 minutes.

Serve with brandy hard sauce.

Keeps in refrigerator for up to 3 days. For longer storage, it should be frozen.

HINT:

— *To freshen stale bread or rolls wrap in a dampened paper towel and MW PL4. (4 rolls approx. 1 minute)*

MUFFINS - HOW TO MICROWAVE

When looking for a microwave muffin pan, look for one with steam vents in the bottom of each muffin space. This allows steam to escape and alleviates the problem of muffins becoming soggy on the bottom.

Use paper liners when making muffins.

If you do not have a muffin pan, place paper liners inside coffee cups set in a ring pattern in the microwave. You can also cut horizontal "slices" from a styrofoam coffee cup to create rings into which you can set the paper liners. The styrofoam rings keep the papers from spreading open during the cooking process. You can also use paper bathroom drinking cups, which incidently pack especially well in brown bag lunches.

If you are using a muffin pan, elevate it off the floor of the oven by placing it on an inverted bowl or empty container.

Cook muffins at FP for 45 seconds each when cooking individually or 2½ minutes, approximately, for a pan of six.

Muffins will appear slightly moist on the surface and will finish cooking during standing time, about 2 minutes.

If there are one or two muffins in a batch that are not quite done, simply return the undercooked ones to the oven and continue cooking for ten seconds at a time.

YEAST BREADS - HOW TO MICROWAVE

Yeast products ferment and proof very quickly in the microwave oven. Bread can be baked in the microwave, but the crust will not brown and the texture will not be as fine as it would be in conventional cooking.

So, my personal choice is to use the microwave for fermenting and proofing, to save time, and then bake the yeast products in a conventional stove.

Always use glass containers for fermenting and proofing. While kneading dough, prepare microwave. Put 2 cups of water in a glass measure and MW FP 5 minutes.

Put kneaded dough in a greased glass bowl, turn over to coat all sides. Cover with a cloth and place bowl of dough in microwave with the water and MW PL1 (lowest setting) for 15 minutes. Dough should double in volume. Fold dough over several times. Shape. Repeat procedure to proof.

You can bake the product in the microwave at this point. For one loaf of bread, MW FP 7 minutes, or until it sounds hollow when tapped. Brown in conventional oven 8 - 10 minutes at 500° Fahrenheit.

As I mentioned before, I prefer to bake my bread conventionally.

BANANA BREAD

1¾ cups all-purpose flour
1½ tsp. baking powder
½ tsp. baking soda
½ tsp. salt
1 c. mashed ripe banana
1 tbsp. lemon juice

¾ c. sugar
⅓ c. margarine or butter
2 eggs
⅓ c. milk
½ c. coarsely chopped walnuts

Lightly grease bottom only of loaf dish, 9 x 5 inches or ring pan. Combine in medium mixing bowl flour, baking powder, baking soda and salt. Set aside. Mix mashed banana and lemon juice. Set aside.

Beat sugar and margarine in a large bowl until light and fluffy. Add eggs, one at a time, beating well after each. Alternately stir in milk and dry ingredients. Fold in walnuts and banana mixture. Pour batter into prepared pan if using loaf pan. Cover ends with 2-inch strips of aluminum foil and mold to fit around handles. Place loaf dish on inverted saucer (or rack) in oven.

MW PL7 for 8 - 10 minutes. Rotate loaf dish quarter turn 2 or 3 times. MW FP until no uncooked batter can be seen through bottom of dish and wooden pick inserted in center comes out clean, 1 - 2 minutes. Cool on countertop 10 minutes. Remove from loaf dish. YIELD: one 9 inch loaf.

BASIC BISCUIT MIX

5 c. flour
3 tbsp. baking powder
1½ tsp. salt

¾ c. margarine or shortening, cut in small pieces

In a mixing bowl, combine half of the flour with baking powder and salt. Cut in margarine or shortening with low speed of mixer or pastry cutter. Particles should be fine. Add remaining flour and mix. Store in covered container and refrigerate or freeze for later use. YIELD: 7½ cups.

BASIC BISCUIT MIX BISCUITS

1 c. basic biscuit mix
¼ - ⅓ c. milk

2 tbsp. margarine, melted
⅓ c. toasted bread crumbs

In mixing bowl, combine basic biscuit mix and milk. Stir only until dough clings together. Knead dough on floured surface about 10 times for lightness and flakiness. Roll or pat out to 1½ inches thick. Cut using 2 inch cutter. Brush with melted margarine, sprinkle with crumbs. Place on pie plate in a circle. MW FP 2 - 4 minutes or until dry and puffy. Rotate dish a half turn every minute. Remove to wire rack immediately.

VARIATION: Add ¼ cup shredded Cheddar cheese to dry mix before adding milk.

BASIC BISCUIT CINNAMON RING

2 c. basic biscuit mix (p. 126)
⅔ c. milk
½ c. sugar

¼ c. graham wafer crumbs
2 tsp. cinnamon
¼ c. butter, melted

VANILLA ICING:
1 tbsp. butter*
1 c. icing sugar

1 - 2 tbsp. milk
¼ tsp. vanilla

Mix sugar, graham wafer crumbs and cinnamon in a bowl. Set aside. Combine biscuit mix with milk and mix until just blended. If dough is too sticky add an extra tablespoon or two of biscuit mix. Roll or pat on a lightly floured surface to ¾ inch thick. Cut in 2 inch rounds. Dip each round in melted butter and then in cinnamon mixture.

Lay rounds in 1-quart ring mold or arrange around edge of pie dish or large plate. Overlap rounds. MW FP 4 - 7 minutes, or until top springs back in several places. Be sure to rotate dish ½ turn after half the time. Do not overbake or they will be hard and dry when they cool. Cool 2 minutes; loosen and turn out onto serving plate. Frost with Vanilla Icing while warm.

VANILLA ICING: *(If you have any melted butter left from dipping the biscuits, use that.) Combine all ingredients until smooth. Drizzle over cinnamon ring.

BASIC BISCUIT RASPBERRY COFFEE CAKE

3 oz. cream cheese
¼ c. butter
2 c. basic biscuit mix (p.126)
⅓ c. milk

½ c. raspberry preserves
Vanilla Icing (see basic biscuit cinnamon ring)

In mixing bowl cut cream cheese and butter into biscuit mix until mixture is crumbly. Blend in milk. Turn dough out onto lightly floured surface and knead 8 - 10 strokes.

On waxed paper, roll dough to form 12 x 18 inch rectangle. Carefully turn onto greased microproof baking sheet. Remove waxed paper.

Spread raspberry preserves evenly down center of dough. Make 2½ inch long slits at 1 inch intervals on long sides of rectangle. Fold each strip over filling.

MW FP 4 - 5 minutes, or until dry looking and puffy. Drizzle warm cake with Vanilla Icing.

After cake is iced sprinkle lightly with cinnamon.

CARAMEL BISCUIT RING

10 oz. pkg. flaky refrigerator biscuits
1 c. brown sugar
½ c. butter or margarine
½ tsp. grated orange peel
½ tsp. cinnamon
½ c. chopped nuts
⅓ c. chopped maraschino cherries (optional)

In a glass bowl MW sugar and butter at PL7 for 1¼ minutes or until melted. Mix in nuts, orange peel, cinnamon and cherries. Spread just enough of this mixture on the bottom of a ring dish to cover. Separate each biscuit into 3 pieces. Place half of the biscuit pieces over the sugar mixture in the ring dish. Spread with half of the remaining sugar mixture. Repeat with remaining biscuit pieces, ending with sugar mixture. MW 5 minutes, covered with waxed paper. Let stand, covered 5 minutes. Do not overcook or the biscuits will become hard and tough.

CARROT MUFFINS

½ c. brown sugar
⅓ c. oil
1 egg
1¼ c. grated carrots
1 c. flour
1 tsp. cinnamon
½ tsp. nutmeg
½ tsp. baking powder
¼ tsp. baking soda
¼ tsp. salt

Mix sugar and oil in medium bowl. Beat in egg. Stir in carrots. Stir in remaining ingredients just until moistened. Line microwave muffin pans with paper liners. Spoon batter into cups, filling half full. For 6 muffins MW FP 2 -3 minutes. After 1 minute of cooking time, turn pan a quarter turn. Continue cooking. When done edges of muffins are firm but centres are still slightly soft. Allow muffins to stand 5 minutes. Repeat this procedure with remaining batter. Serve warm. YIELD: 12 muffins.

MINCEMEAT MUFFINS

¾ c. vegetable oil
1 c. white or brown sugar
2 eggs, beaten
¾ c. milk
1 c. bran
1 c. mincemeat
2 c. all-purpose flour
2 tsp. baking powder
1 tsp. salt
1 tsp. baking soda

Combine liquid ingredients in a large bowl. Add bran and mincemeat. Sift dry ingredients into liquid ingredients and stir to moisten. This mixture can be stored in the fridge until needed. Fill muffin cups half full with batter. Cook: 1 muffin 30 - 45 seconds, 2 muffins 45 seconds to 1¼ minutes, 4 muffins 1¼ - 1¾ minutes, 6 muffins 1¾ - 2¼ minutes. Cover and let stand 2 minutes.

PUMPKIN MUFFINS

Because of the natural color of this batter, it is most suitable for microwaving.

4	eggs	½	tsp. nutmeg
2	c. white sugar	¼	tsp. cloves
1½	c. melted margarine	2	tsp. baking soda
1½	c. cooked pumpkin	2	tsp. baking powder
3	c. flour	1	tsp. salt
1½	tbsp. cinnamon	¾	c. walnut or pecan pieces
1	tsp. ginger		

Whisk eggs well. Whisk in sugar, margarine and pumpkin. Mix well. Sift all dry ingredients together and add to wet ingredients. Add nuts. Gently stir to moisten batter. Cook six muffins at a time. Elevate muffin rack and MW FP 2 - 2½ minutes. YIELD: 24 muffins.

REFRIGERATOR BRAN MUFFINS

4	c. whole-wheat flour	1	c. raisins
3	c. natural bran	4	eggs
¾	c. brown sugar	¾	c. vegetable oil
1	tsp. salt	1½	c. molasses
2	tsp. baking soda	2¼	c. buttermilk or sour milk

NUT SPICE TOPPING: ¾ c. chopped walnuts
¾ c. brown sugar   1½ tsp. cinnamon

TOPPING: Place ingredients in jar and shake to blend.

MUFFINS: In large bowl, thoroughly combine flour, bran, sugar, salt, baking soda and raisins. Beat eggs in medium bowl. Beat in oil, molasses and buttermilk. Pour liquid ingredients over bran mixture. Blend gently but thoroughly. Refrigerate 24 hours before use.

When ready to use, spoon batter into medium sized paper baking cups placed in 6-ounce custard cups, or microwave muffin pan. Fill each cup half full. Sprinkle a teaspoon of Nut Spice Topping on each muffin.

Microwave with FP until no longer doughy, rotating cups once: 1 muffin (½ - ¾ minute), 2 muffins (¾ - 1¼ minutes), 4 muffins (1¼ - 1¾ minutes), 6 muffins (1¾ - 2¼ minutes).

Remove muffins immediately to cooling rack and let stand 2 minutes before serving. Makes approximately 5 dozen muffins. May be stored in refrigerator up to one month.

RAISIN BRAN MUFFINS

2¼ c. raisin bran cereal	⅔ c. flour
⅔ c. milk	6 tbsp. packed brown sugar
6 tbsp. oil	1 tbsp. baking powder
2 eggs, beaten	½ tsp. cinnamon

Combine cereal, milk, oil and eggs. Stir until cereal is moistened. Let stand 5 minutes. Combine flour, sugar, baking powder and cinnamon. Add to cereal mixture; stir until well blended.

Line 6-cup muffin pan with paper baking cups; fill ⅔ full. MW PL6 for 5½ - 6½ minutes until toothpick inserted near centre comes out clean. Let stand 5 minutes. Repeat procedure with remaining batter. Serve warm. YIELD: 12 muffins.

SAVORY CHEESE BREAD

2 c. all-purpose flour	½ c. shredded Cheddar
1 tbsp. dry onion flakes	cheese
2 tsp. poppy seed	¼ c. plus 2 tbsp. butter
2 tsp. sugar	or margarine
1½ tsp. baking powder	⅔ c. buttermilk or sour milk*
½ tsp. soda	1 egg, slightly beaten
½ tsp. salt	

*To sour milk, combine 1 tablespoon lemon juice or vinegar with enough milk to measure ⅔ cup.

TOPPING:

1 tsp. butter or margarine, melted	2 tbsp. grated Parmesan cheese
2 tbsp. dry bread crumbs	1 tsp. poppy seed

TOPPING: Combine topping ingredients until crumbly.

Combine in mixing bowl, flour, onion flakes, poppy seeds, sugar, baking powder, soda, salt and cheese. Cut in butter at low speed of mixer or with pastry blender until particles are fine. Stir in buttermilk and egg until well blended.

Turn into 9 inch pie plate or 10 inch tube baking dish which has been lightly greased, then lined with waxed paper. Shape into rounded loaf with spoon. Sprinkle with topping. Make several ½-inch deep crisscross cuts across top with sharp knife.

MW PL5 for 6 minutes, rotating ½ turn every 3 minutes. MW FP 3 - 6 minutes, or until no longer doughy in center, rotating ½ turn every 2 minutes. Let stand 10 minutes. Serve warm or cold, cut into thin wedges or slices. YIELD: 9 or 10 inch round loaf.

SOUR CREAM BRUNCH CAKE

⅔ c. sugar
⅓ c. margarine or butter, softened
⅔ c. dairy sour cream
2 eggs
1⅓ c. all-purpose flour
½ tsp. baking soda

½ tsp. baking powder
½ tsp. salt
¼ c. margarine or butter
⅓ c. packed brown sugar
¾ tsp. ground cinnamon
½ c. chopped nuts

Beat sugar and ⅓ cup margarine until light and fluffy. Beat in sour cream and eggs until smooth. Add flour, baking soda, baking powder and salt. Beat at medium speed of electric mixer 2 - 3 minutes. Set batter aside.

Place ¼ cup margarine in round baking dish, 9 x 1½ inches. MW FP until melted, 45 seconds to 1 minute 15 seconds. Mix brown sugar and cinnamon; sprinkle over margarine. Sprinkle nuts over brown sugar. Gently spread batter in baking dish. Elevate dish on rack or inverted bowl.

MW PL7 until wooden pick inserted in center comes out clean, 6 - 9 minutes. Let stand 3 minutes to cool. Invert onto serving plate. YIELD: 9 inch cake.

EXTRA RECIPES

EXTRA RECIPES

VEGETABLES

VEGETABLES - HOW TO MICROWAVE

The microwave oven is the perfect answer to cooking nutritious, delicious vegetables. Because there is little or no water required to cook the vegetables, they retain most of their valuable nutrients.

Vegetables are generally cooked at Full Power for about 7 minutes per pound.

It is imperative to pierce the skins of vegetables which have skins as the steam from the moisture within the vegetable builds up under the skin and can cause the vegetable to "explode" in the oven. A good example of this disaster is a potato.

Root vegetables will require the addition of water, but generally no more than about ¼ of a cup. Other vegetables such as broccoli and cauliflower simply use the water that is left on their surface during the washing process.

Placement of the vegetables is important - the thicker, more dense portion of the vegetable should point toward the outside of the cooking vessel, i.e. broccoli should be placed with the flowerheads pointing to the centre and the stem ends out in a spoke fashion. Be sure to cut the pieces in uniform sizes to ensure even cooking.

When preparing vegetables for stew or a mixed dish, cut more quickly cooking vegetables in larger pieces than those that take longer to cook. For example if cooking broccoli and carrots together cut the carrots into fairly thin coins and leave the broccoli in fairly large pieces.

Unless they have a skin, vegetables should be cooked covered tightly with plastic wrap, venting back one corner to allow excess steam to escape, or a tight fitting lid.

Salt vegetables after cooking, or be sure to dissolve salt in liquid.

Corn ears can be successfully cooked in their natural husks. Simply peel back the husk, remove any unwanted "livestock" and cornsilk, re-cover and MW FP 4 - 4½ minutes per ear. When you remove the husk you will want to use an oven mitt or pot holder as it will be very hot to handle.

If baking potatoes, be sure to turn over and rearrange halfway through cooking time. Wrap baked potatoes in foil to retain heat and they will keep hot up to half hour.

ARTICHOKES WITH MUSTARD SAUCE

4   med. artichokes
¼   c. water
½   c. prepared brown
    mustard

¼   c. mayonnaise or
    salad dressing
1   tbsp. horseradish sauce
    (optional)

Slice 1 inch from top of artichokes; trim stem even with base. Cut off sharp tips of outer leaves. Rinse artichokes under cold water. Arrange in upright position in square baking dish, 8 x 8 inches. Pour ¼ cup water into baking dish. Cover with plastic wrap.

MW FP 10 - 16 minutes until lower leaves can be pulled off with a slight tug and base is fork-tender. Rotate baking dish and re-arrange artichokes 2 to 3 times during cooking. Mix remaining ingredients. Serve with artichokes. YIELD: 4 servings.

BEETS 'N' PINEAPPLE

3   med. beets, cooked,
    peeled & sliced
2   tsp. cornstarch

14 oz. can pineapple chunks,
    drained; reserve juice
¼   c. orange or apple juice

Place cooked sliced beets and pineapple chunks in a casserole.

Dissolve cornstarch in pineapple juice and add orange or apple juice. Pour over beets and pineapple chunks. Place in microwave; MW FP 3 - 5 minutes or until heated through and sauce is thickened; stir occasionally. YIELD: 6 servings.

BEETS 'N' HONEY

1   tbsp. cornstarch
½   tsp. salt
1   tbsp. water or beet juice
2   tbsp. vinegar

¼   c. honey
1   tbsp. butter or margarine
2   c. diced or sliced,
    cooked beets

In a small glass bowl or measuring cup combine cornstarch and salt. Blend in water or beet juice. Add vinegar, honey and butter. MW FP 1¼ minutes or until thickened. Stir 3 or 4 times during cooking. Add sauce to beets in a 1½-quart covered casserole. MW FP 1½ minutes. Let stand about 10 minutes to blend flavors. Reheat. YIELD: 4 - 6 servings.

ASPARAGUS SCALLOP

2 - 10 oz. pkgs. frozen cut asparagus
2 tbsp. water
2 tbsp. margarine or butter
¼ c. slivered almonds
1 tbsp. margarine or butter
1 tbsp. all-purpose flour
¼ tsp. salt
½ c. milk
½ c. shredded sharp Cheddar cheese (about 2 oz.)

Place asparagus and water in 1½-quart casserole; cover. MW FP 8 - 10 minutes or until heated through, stirring to break apart after half the time. Drain and set aside.

Place 2 tablespoons margarine in small bowl. MW FP 45 seconds or until melted. Mix in almonds to coat. MW FP 2 - 3 minutes or until light brown. Set aside.

Place 1 tablespoon margarine in small bowl or 2-cup measure. MW FP 45 seconds or until melted. Stir in flour and salt. Blend in milk. MW PL7 until thickened, 2 - 3½ minutes, stirring every 30 seconds to 1 minute. Stir in cheese until melted. Pour over asparagus. Sprinkle with almonds. MW PL7 until heated through, 2 - 3 minutes. YIELD: 4 - 6 servings.

HINT:
— *Stamp collectors can remove stamps by putting a drop of water on the stamp to be removed from the paper and MW FP 20 seconds.*

ASPARAGUS TIMBALE

¼ c. finely minced onions
2 tsp. butter
White pepper to taste
¼ tsp. nutmeg
½ c. grated Swiss cheese
⅓ c. dry bread crumbs
3 eggs
1 c. light cream
1½ c. asparagus cut into ½-inch pieces*

* When using fresh asparagus, MW FP 3 - 4 minutes. For frozen asparagus, simply thaw. Slice and use without cooking. Save a few spears for garnish.

Grease a 5-cup microproof savarin ring mold with butter. Sprinkle with cereal or browned bread crumbs. Combine onions and butter in a medium sized microproof bowl. MW FP 1 minute. Stir in pepper, nutmeg, cheese and bread crumbs.

Beat in eggs. Put cream in glass measuring cup. MW FP 40 - 60 seconds. Beat warmed cream into egg-cheese mixture. Fold in asparagus pieces.

Pour into mold and cover with wax paper. MW PL4 for 13 - 15 minutes until custard is set. Allow to stand 8 minutes after removing from oven. (N.B. To make individual timbales in 4-ounce ramekins, MW 2 - 2½ minutes per ramekin.)

BEETS, SWEET & SOUR STYLE

14 oz. can diced beets, drained	⅓ c. cider vinegar
4 tsp. cornstarch	⅓ c. water
½ c. sugar	3 tbsp. butter
	Salt and pepper to taste

Place drained beets in a 2-quart casserole dish. In small bowl combine cornstarch, sugar, cider, vinegar, water and butter. Mix thoroughly. Cover sauce with plastic wrap. MW FP 3 minutes. Stir well. MW FP another 3 minutes or until sauce is creamy and transparent. Pour sauce over beets. Stir well. MW FP 2 - 3 minutes or until hot. Season to taste with salt and pepper. YIELD: 4 - 6 servings.

BROCCOLI CHEESE SUNBURST

1½ lbs. fresh broccoli	1 tsp. prepared mustard
2 tbsp. water	½ c. shredded Cheddar cheese
½ c. mayonnaise or salad dressing	Paprika
1 tsp. onion, chopped fine	

Place broccoli in 1½-quart glass casserole. Arrange with stalk ends to outside of dish. Add water. Cover with glass lid or plastic wrap. MW FP 6 - 8 minutes or until tender crisp. Turn broccoli over halfway through cooking time.

Combine mayonnaise, onion, mustard and cheese in small mixing bowl. MW PL6 2 - 4 minutes or until cheese is melted. Stir after first 2 minutes. Arrange broccoli in dish with florets to outside edge. Pour cheese sauce over centre, leaving florets exposed. Sprinkle with paprika. Let stand 2 minutes before serving. YIELD: 6 - 8 servings.

BOSTON BAKED BEANS

28 oz. baked beans	4 med. tomatoes, diced
8 slices cooked bacon, crumbled	1 med. onion, diced
	3 tbsp. demerara sugar

Combine all ingredients in a 2-quart casserole with lid. Cover and MW FP 10 minutes or until slightly bubbly, stirring twice during cooking time. Let stand 3 - 5 minutes.

BROCCOLI IN LEMON SAUCE

2 - 10 oz. pkgs. frozen broccoli spears	1 tbsp. all-purpose flour
2 tbsp. water	½ c. milk
2 tbsp. margarine or butter	2 tsp. lemon zest
	⅛ tsp. salt

Place broccoli and water in 2-quart casserole; cover. MW FP until heated through, 8 - 12 minutes, stirring to break apart after half the time. Drain and set aside.

Place margarine in small bowl or 2-cup measure. MW FP until melted, 30 seconds to 1 minute. Stir in flour. Blend in remaining ingredients. MW PL7 until thickened, 2½ - 3 minutes, stirring every 30 seconds to 1 minute. Pour over broccoli. MW PL7 until heated through, 2 - 3 minutes. YIELD: 4 - 6 servings.

BROCCOLI SPECIAL

2 tbsp. minced onion	½ tsp. paprika
2 tbsp. butter	⅛ tsp. salt
1 ½ c. sour cream	Dash pepper
2 tbsp. sugar	2 - 10 oz. pkgs. broccoli, cooked
1 tsp. vinegar	
½ tsp. poppy seed	⅓ c. chopped cashews

Put onion and butter in 1-quart casserole. MW FP for 2 minutes. Stir. Mix in sour cream, sugar, vinegar, poppy seed, paprika, salt and pepper. MW FP 2 minutes. Stir halfway through cooking time. Pour sauce over broccoli. Top with cashews. YIELD: 6 - 8 servings.

CARROT COINS IN GLAZE

4 lge. carrots (1 lb.)	1 tbsp. water
3 tbsp. packed brown sugar	½ tsp. salt
2 tbsp. margarine or butter	⅛ tsp. ground cinnamon

Cut carrots into thin coins. Set aside. Combine brown sugar, margarine, water, salt and cinnamon in 1½-quart casserole.

MW FP until margarine is melted, 45 seconds to 1 minute 30 seconds. Stir to blend. Stir in carrots until coated. Cover. MW FP until carrots are tender, 5 - 8 minutes, stirring once. YIELD: 4 - 6 servings.

CARROT STRIPS 'N' SPICE

4	c. carrots strips	2	drops Tabasco sauce
2	tbsp. butter		Salt
1	tsp. dry mustard	2	tbsp. brown sugar

Cut carrots in 2-inch strips. Place in 1½-quart casserole with butter. MW FP 5 minutes. Stir halfway through cooking time. Combine brown sugar, mustard and Tabasco sauce. Pour over carrots. MW FP 5 minutes or until tender. Stir halfway through cooking time. Season to taste. YIELD: 4 servings.

CARROTS, GINGERED

3	tbsp. butter	2	oranges, peeled & sectioned
1	tbsp. brown sugar		
½	tsp. salt	1	lb. carrots, peeled & cut in (2-inch chunks) or coins
¼	tsp. ground ginger		

Put butter in a 1-quart covered casserole and MW FP 45 seconds or until melted. Mix in brown sugar and spices. Add carrots and orange sections, mixing until coated. MW FP 7 minutes until carrots are tender, stirring once during cooking time. Let stand, covered, 1 - 2 minutes.

CARROTS IN CINNAMON GLAZE

4	c. peeled & sliced carrots	¼	c. boiling water
⅓	c. honey	1	tsp. cinnamon
⅓	c. butter		Grated rind of 1 lemon
2	tbsp. brown sugar		Salt & pepper to taste
4	tbsp. vegetable oil		

Place all ingredients except carrots in a 2-quart casserole. Do not cover. MW FP 2 minutes. Add carrots. MW FP, uncovered, another 16 minutes, stirring twice. Drain. Let stand 2 - 3 minutes. YIELD: 4 - 6 servings.

CARROTS IN ORANGE GLAZE

2	c. julienned carrots	1	tbsp. butter
¼	c. orange juice	1	tbsp. chopped fresh mint
1	tsp. cornstarch		

Combine all ingredients except mint in a 1-quart (1.5 L) microwave ovenproof casserole. Cover. MW FP 7 - 9 minutes, stirring once. Stir in mint and allow to stand 3 minutes before serving. YIELD: 4 - 6 servings.

CARROTS WITH A SQUEEZE OF ORANGE

4	lge. carrots (1 lb.), cut in thin slices	1	tbsp. grated orange zest
¼	c. margarine or butter	1	tsp. sugar
		2	tbsp. orange juice

Combine ingredients in a 1-quart casserole. Cover. MW FP 4 - 6 minutes or until carrots are tender.

Shake casserole after 3 minutes to coat carrots. Let stand, covered, 5 minutes. Shake casserole before serving. YIELD: 4 - 6 servings.

CAULIFLOWER/BROCCOLI PLATE WITH CHEESE SAUCE

½	lb. fresh cauliflower	1	sliced carrot
½	lb. fresh broccoli		

Wash, but do not dry vegetables. Break into flowerets and arrange on a platter with denser parts of the vegetables toward the outside of the platter, in a ring pattern.

Scatter with carrot slices. Cover tightly with plastic wrap, venting at one side. MW FP 7 minutes. Let stand, covered, for 10 minutes. Prepare sauce while vegetables are standing.

CHEESE SAUCE FOR VEGETABLES

1	tbsp. butter	½	c. grated Cheddar cheese
1	tbsp. flour	½	tsp. seasoned salt
½	c. milk		

Put butter in a 2-cup measure. MW FP 45 seconds or until butter is melted. Whisk in flour to make a paste. Add milk, whisking constantly.

MW FP 2 minutes, whisking once or twice during cooking to avoid lumping. Remove from oven and add cheese and seasoned salt and whisk to blend melting cheese. Pour over vegetables when well blended.

CARROT SUNRISE

1½ c. frozen whole baby carrots		2	tsp. instant orange breakfast drink mix, divided

Place carrots in 1-quart casserole. Sprinkle with 1 teaspoon drink mix; cover. MW FP for 5 - 7 minutes, or until carrots are fork tender. Drain.

Sprinkle with remaining 1 teaspoon drink mix. Stir to coat. Let stand covered, 5 minutes.

CAULIFLOWER AU GRATIN

1 med. head cauliflower (about 1 lb.), separated into flowerets	1 tsp. prepared mustard (optional)
2 tbsp. water	¼ tsp. salt
1 tbsp. margarine or butter	½ c. shredded Cheddar cheese (about 2 oz.)
1 tbsp. all-purpose flour	⅛ tsp. paprika
½ c. milk	

Place cauliflowerets and water in 1-quart casserole; cover. MW FP until tender, 7 - 10 minutes, stirring after half the cooking time. Drain and set aside.

Place margarine in 2-cup measure. MW FP until melted, 30 seconds to 1 minute. Stir in flour. Blend in milk, mustard and salt. MW PL7 until thickened, 2 - 5 minutes, stirring every minute. Stir in cheese until melted. Pour over cauliflowerets; sprinkle with paprika. YIELD: 4 servings.

CHEESY CABBAGE CASSEROLE

1 small cabbage, shredded	2 tbsp. margarine
½ tsp. salt	⅛ tsp. nutmeg
¼ c. milk	½ c. shredded Cheddar cheese
¼ c. chopped onion	

Combine cabbage, salt, milk, onion, butter and nutmeg in 2-quart casserole. Cover. MW FP 5 minutes. Stir. MW FP 5 minutes longer or until tender-crisp. Stir in cheese. MW FP 2 minutes. Let stand, covered, 2 minutes. YIELD: 4 servings.

CAULIFLOWER ORIENTAL

1 med. head cauliflower	1 beef or chicken bouillon cube
½ c. chopped onion	
½ c. diced celery	1 tbsp. cornstarch
3 sprigs chopped parsley	1 tbsp. soya sauce
1 tbsp. butter or margarine	Dash pepper
1 c. hot water	

Wash cauliflower. Remove outer green stalks. Place in 2-quart covered casserole. MW FP 10 minutes. Drain. In 1½-pint ceramic dish, combine onion, celery, parsley and butter. MW FP 5 minutes. Stir halfway through cooking time.

Dissolve bouillon cube in water. Blend in cornstarch, soya sauce and pepper. Pour into onion mixture. MW FP 2 minutes. Stir every 30 seconds. Place cooked cauliflower head on serving dish. Top with sauce. YIELD: 6 servings.

CAULIFLOWER SCRAMBLE

2 - 10 oz. pkgs. cauliflower in cheese sauce
1 med. zucchini, thinly sliced
¼ c. chopped onion
2 tbsp. margarine or butter
2 med. tomatoes, each cut into 8 wedges
½ tsp. salt
¼ tsp. dried thyme leaves

Remove cauliflower pouches from boxes. Place both pouches in oven. MW FP until thawed but not hot, 4 - 6 minutes. Re-arrange pouches once. Set aside.

Combine zucchini, onion and margarine in 2-quart casserole. MW FP until vegetables are tender-crisp, 2½ - 4 minutes. Stir in cauliflower, tomatoes, salt and thyme. MW FP 4½ - 6½ minutes, covered, until heated through. Stir before serving. YIELD: 4 - 6 servings.

CELERY AMANDINE

2 tbsp. butter
4 c. diagonally-sliced celery
1 tsp. chicken broth powder
⅛ tsp. garlic powder
½ tsp. sugar
⅛ tsp. ground ginger
1 tbsp. instant minced onions
⅓ c. blanched whole almonds or slivers

Put butter in a 2-quart casserole. MW FP 1 minute or until melted. Add all the ingredients except the almonds. Cover, MW FP 7 minutes. Stir occasionally. Add almonds. Microwave one more minute. YIELD: 4 servings.

CORN-STUFFED TOMATOES

6 med. tomatoes
Salt
10 oz. pkg. frozen cut corn, defrosted
2 tbsp. butter
¼ c. chopped green onion
½ tsp. salt
⅛ tsp. pepper
2 tbsp. bread crumbs
¼ c. Parmesan cheese

Cut off tops of tomatoes. Scoop out the pulp. This is easy with a melon baller or grapefruit knife. Salt the insides of the shells. Turn over to drain.

Put remaining ingredients in a small bowl. MW FP 2 minutes, stirring after 1 minute.

Fill tomatoes. Place on a serving dish. MW FP 4 - 5 minutes until warm. If made ahead and refrigerated, add one minute to the final microwave time. YIELD: 6 servings.

CAULIFLOWER WITH PIMIENTO COTTAGE CHEESE SAUCE

1 head cauliflower, (1½ lbs.)	½ c. shredded sharp Cheddar cheese
¼ c. water	1 - 2 oz. jar chopped pimiento, undrained
1 tbsp. butter	
1 tbsp. all-purpose flour	½ tsp. dried dill weed
½ c. milk	½ tsp. salt
1 c. small curd cottage cheese	⅛ tsp. ground black pepper

Trim green leaves from cauliflower and remove core leaving head intact. Place cauliflower in 1½-quart microwave casserole. Add water. Cover with plastic wrap, MW FP 7 -11 minutes, rotating ½ turn after 4 minutes, until cauliflower is tender. Set aside, covered.

Meanwhile, in a 1-quart microwave mixing bowl or casserole, place butter and flour. MW FP about 2 minutes, whisking after 1 minute, until butter and flour mixture is well combined. Add milk, MW FP 2 - 5 minutes longer, whisking every minute, until sauce is boiling, thickened and smooth.

Stir in cottage cheese, Cheddar cheese, pimiento, dill weed, salt and pepper. MW FP 2 - 4 additional minutes, just until cheeses are partially melted and sauce is hot and well combined.

Transfer cauliflower to serving plate, and spoon some of the sauce over top. Cut cauliflower in wedges to serve and pass additional sauce at table. YIELD: 6 servings.

EGGPLANT ITALIANO

1 med. eggplant	1 tsp. oregano
2 tbsp. butter or margarine	1 tsp. basil
1 c. chopped onion	1 clove garlic, minced
1 green pepper, chopped	½ tsp. salt
1 lb. can tomatoes, partially drained	⅛ tsp. pepper
	3 slices Mozzarella cheese

Cut eggplant in half lengthwise. Scoop out pulp leaving shell about ½ an inch thick. Chop eggplant pulp coarsely. Place butter in an 8 x 8 inch microproof dish. MW FP 45 seconds or until butter is melted. Add onion and green pepper. MW FP 3 minutes or until onion is transparent and pepper is tender. Add eggplant, tomatoes and seasonings. Cover. MW FP 6 minutes until eggplant is tender, stirring after 3 minutes. Drain excess juices. Fill eggplant shells with vegetable mixture. Top with cheese. MW PL7 for 2 minutes or until cheese is melted.

GREEN BEANS SHERYN

10 oz. box French style green beans	½ c. diced red pepper
⅛ c. salad oil	½ tsp. salt
1 clove garlic, crushed	½ tsp. basil
1 tbsp. chopped onion	¼ c. Parmesan cheese

Put box of beans into oven and MW FP 6 minutes. Set aside. Put oil and garlic in a covered casserole and MW FP 1 minute. Stir. Add onion and red pepper and MW FP 1 minute. Add green beans and spices and half of the cheese and MW FP 1 minute. Let stand 2 minutes. Sprinkle with remaining cheese, toss and serve.

GREEN BEAN AND ONION QUICK CASSEROLE

10 oz. pkg. frozen, cut green beans	4 oz. can pimiento, chopped
3 tbsp. butter or margarine	2 tsp. prepared mustard
1 med. onion, finely chopped	7½ oz. can Spanish-style tomato sauce
Pinch garlic salt	1½ c. shredded Cheddar cheese
½ green pepper, seeded & cut in cubes	Salt & Pepper

Put green beans in covered glass casserole dish. Do not add water. MW FP 6 - 7 minutes. Drain. Set aside. Put butter in 1½-quart glass casserole. MW FP 30 seconds. Add onion, garlic, salt, green pepper and pimiento. Cover. MW FP until tender, for 2 - 3 minutes. Stir in mustard, tomato sauce and cheese. Add beans to tomato sauce mixture. MW FP, covered, 4 - 5 minutes. YIELD: 3 - 4 servings.

GREEN BEANS SWEET & SOUR

3 slices bacon, cut up	¼ tsp. dry mustard
1 small onion, sliced & separated into rings	2 tbsp. vinegar
2 tbsp. packed brown sugar	16 oz. frozen French-style green beans
½ tsp. salt	

Place bacon and onion in small bowl. MW FP 2 - 3 minutes, or until onion is tender and bacon cooked, stirring once. Mix in brown sugar, salt, mustard and vinegar.

Place green beans in 2-quart casserole. Cover with plastic wrap. MW FP 6 - 8 minutes, or until heated, stirring after half the time. Drain. Add bacon-onion mixture, tossing to combine. MW FP 2 - 3 minutes, or until heated.

GREEN BEANS WITH WALNUT SAUCE

1	lb. fresh green beans, strings removed, cut into 1-inch pieces or	3	tbsp. scallions, minced
		½	tsp. peeled & minced garlic
2 -	10 oz. pkgs. frozen green beans	1	tbsp. ketchup
	Water	1	tsp. salt
		2	tbsp. tarragon vinegar
½	c. chicken broth	½	c. finely chopped walnuts

In a 1½-quart microwave casserole, place beans. For fresh beans, add ½ cup water. Cover. MW FP 9 - 13 minutes, stirring every 4 minutes, until beans lose raw taste.

For frozen beans, add 2 tablespoons water. MW FP 6 - 10 minutes, breaking up after 2 minutes, until tender and bright green.

Remove and let stand, covered.

Meanwhile in a 2 to 4 cup microwave casserole or bowl, place chicken broth, scallions, garlic, ketchup, salt and vinegar. MW FP 1 - 3 minutes, just until steaming hot.

Stir in walnuts. Add sauce to beans and toss to combine. YIELD: 4 servings.

JAPANESE VEGETABLES

2	stalks celery, cut on bias	3	green onions, fanned
2	stalks broccoli	1	tomato
1	green pepper	¼	lb. mushrooms

TERIYAKI SAUCE:

1	tbsp. vegetable oil	½	tsp. ginger
1	tbsp. soya sauce	½	tsp. sugar
1	clove garlic	½	c. water

On a large plate or baking dish, arrange vegetables in a circular fashion with the densest vegetable on the outside of the ring, and the least dense to the centre. (Celery, broccoli-stem end facing towards outer edge, green pepper, mushrooms, with tomato in centre.) Place fanned green onions on top of arranged vegetables.

In small bowl, combine remaining ingredients. Pour over arranged vegetables. Cover tightly with plastic wrap, venting one edge to allow excess steam to escape. MW FP for approx. 2½ minutes, or until vegetables are tender-crisp.

(Note: The amount of vegetables prepared will affect the amount of time required to microwave this dish.)

ONION AND GREEN PEA CASSEROLE

2 - 14 oz. cans whole white	1	c. frozen peas
onions	½	c. finely chopped celery
Pimiento		(optional)
2	c. med. white sauce	

Gently remove the inside of each onion. Fill hollow with a strip of pimiento. Place onions in casserole dish.

Make medium white sauce. Add peas and celery. Pour sauce mixture over onions. Cover. MW FP 8 minutes or until mixture bubbles. Let stand 2 minutes before serving.

NOTE: This recipe may be made ahead of time and refrigerated until ready to serve. Cook 12 minutes instead of 8 minutes in microwave oven.

ONION CHRYSANTHEMUMS BASTED WITH BOURBON

4	strips bacon	¼	c. bourbon or water
4	med. white or yellow	8	tsp. grated Parmesan
	onions		cheese

In 12 x 8 inch Microwave dish, arrange bacon slices. Cover with waxed paper. MW FP 3 - 6 minutes, until very crisp. Drain bacon on paper towels. Pour bacon fat into small bowl or cup and reserve bacon dish.

Meanwhile, peel onions and remove thin slice from bottoms so onions will sit flat. On cutting board with very sharp knife, make 5 - 6 parallel vertical cuts through each onion, cutting almost through to bottoms.

Then, at right angles to cuts, make 5 or 6 more vertical cuts. At this point, top of onion should look as though it's been cut into squares.

Arrange onions in reserved bacon dish and baste each with reserved bacon fat and 1 tablespoon bourbon. Sprinkle Parmesan cheese over top.

Cover with waxed paper. MW FP 7 - 9 minutes, depending on size of onions, until softened and onions begin to open into flower shape.

Let stand several minutes, then carefully use wide spatula to transfer to serving plate.

Baste with pan juices, and sprinkle each flower with crumbled bacon. YIELD: 4 servings.

PEAS AND ONIONS

10	oz. pkg. frozen peas	¼	c. dry bread crumbs
10	oz. pkg. frozen onions in cream sauce	½	tsp. dried parsley flakes
¼	tsp. salt	2	tbsp. sliced, toasted almonds
2	tbsp. butter or margarine	⅛	tsp. nutmeg

Combine peas and onions in 1½-quart casserole. Add 2 tbsp. water to sauce. Mix. Pour over vegetables. MW FP, covered, 10 - 12 minutes or until hot, stirring once. Stir in salt and nutmeg. Set aside.

Put butter in small glass dish. MW FP 45 seconds or until melted. Stir in bread crumbs, parsley and nuts. Sprinkle over peas and onions. MW FP, uncovered, 1 - 2 minutes or until hot. YIELD: 6 - 8 servings.

PEAS PLUS

2	tbsp. water	3	tbsp. mayonnaise
10	oz. pkg. green peas	¼	tsp. salt
1	carrot, grated	¼	tsp. curry powder
10	tiny pickled pearl onions	1	tsp. sugar

Put water in a 1½-quart casserole. Mix in vegetables. MW FP 5 - 8 minutes or until carrot is tender crisp. Add balance of ingredients. Toss to coat vegetables. YIELD: 4 servings.

POTATO BAKE A LA HELGA

Helga Hawchuk is one of the busiest people I know. Aside from duties as wife and Mother of two beautiful youngsters, Cindy and Andrew, Helga serves on various committees, assists her husband in their family business, is always doing a favor for a friend or neighbor, and is usually serving up an extra plate at dinnertime - often for my son!

If Helga gives you a recipe and says it's quick and delicious, you have to believe her, because not only is she busy, but a great cook too! For the dill used in this recipe Helga freezes a supply of fresh dill in the fall and always has "fresh" dill on hand.

3	potatoes	¼	c. butter
1	onion, finely chopped	½	c. grated Cheddar cheese
	Salt & pepper to taste		Paprika
	Dill to taste		

Peel and cube potatoes into ½-inch chunks. Toss with onion in a buttered casserole. Generously dot with butter or margarine. Season with salt and pepper. Sprinkle with chopped dill. Cover. MW FP 10 - 12 minutes or until potatoes are tender. Sprinkle with cheese and paprika. Let stand, covered, 3 - 5 minutes or until cheese melts. If you wish to have a crispy topping, put the cheese topped casserole under the broiler for a minute or two.

POTATO BOATS

4	potatoes (approx. 7 oz. each)		Salt & pepper
2	tbsp. butter	½	c. shredded sharp cheese
1	c. milk		Paprika

Select four uniform, medium-sized baking potatoes; scrub well. Pierce each potato all the way through with a large fork. Arrange potatoes on paper towel in a ring pattern. Leave about 1-inch space between potatoes.

MW FP for 8 minutes. Turn potatoes over. MW FP an additional 8 minutes. Time varies according to size and variety of potatoes. If potatoes feel slightly firm after recommended cooking time, allow a few minutes standing time. Potatoes will finish cooking on their own.

Let stand a few minutes to cool. Cut thin slice through skin from top of each potato. Scoop out potato from skins, leaving thin, unbroken shell from each potato. Mash potatoes.

Stir in butter, milk, salt and pepper. Whip until potato mixture is light & fluffy. Lightly spoon potato mixture back into shells. Top each potato with cheese. Sprinkle with paprika. Place potatoes in a circle on paper towel. MW FP 5 minutes. If desired, stuffed potatoes may be prepared ahead and refrigerated. Heat in MW 6 - 7 minutes.

POTATO CASSEROLE

1½	c. hot milk	½	tsp. savory
4	med. potatoes, thinly sliced	1	med. onion, chopped
2	tbsp. flour	2	tbsp. butter
2	tsp. salt	1	tsp. paprika
		1	tbsp. chopped parsley

Put milk in 4-cup glass measure. MW FP 3 minutes. Combine potatoes, flour, salt, savory and onion in large casserole. Dot with butter. MW FP, covered, 15 minutes. Stir 3 times during cooking period. Sprinkle top with paprika and chopped parsley. Allow to stand covered 10 minutes to complete the cooking. YIELD: 5 servings.

HINT:

— *To remove odours from oven, squeeze the juice of a lemon into a 1 cup measure and fill with water to 1 cup. MW FP 4 to 5 minutes.*

POTATO ROSETTES

4	potatoes, peeled	3	tbsp. white pepper
	& quartered	3	tbsp. milk
¼	c. water		Salt to taste
1	egg yolk		

Put potatoes in covered microproof casserole. MW FP 8 - 11 minutes, stirring once. Stand 5 minutes. Drain. Whip potatoes. Add egg yolk, milk and salt to taste.

Fit a pastry bag with fluted tip. Fill bag and pipe rosettes on waxed paper or directly on serving platter. To reheat, MW FP 30 - 60 seconds per rosette.

POTATO SOUFFLE

4	med. sized potatoes	1	small onion,
2	tbsp. milk		finely chopped
8	oz. cream cheese	2	eggs
	Salt & pepper to taste		Paprika

Peel, quarter, and rinse potatoes. Add potatoes and water to a casserole. MW FP 7 minutes, or until potatoes are tender. Drain, mash with milk and add salt and pepper to taste. To soften cream cheese MW PL2 for 1 minute. Add softened cream cheese to mashed potatoes. Add eggs and onion and beat until fluffy. Butter a ring mold. MW PL3 for 9 minutes. Sprinkle with paprika. YIELD: 4 - 6 servings.

POTATOES AND PARSLEY

6	med. red potatoes (about	1	tbsp. dried parsley flakes
	2½ lb.) peeled & quartered	½	tsp. salt
¼	c. water	⅛	tsp. pepper
¼	c. margarine or butter		

Place potatoes and water in 2-quart casserole; cover. MW FP 12 - 15 minutes until fork tender, stirring after half the time. Let stand 5 minutes. Drain and set aside.

Place margarine in 2-cup measure. MW FP 1 - 1½ minutes. Stir in remaining ingredients. Pour over potatoes. Toss to coat. YIELD: 4 - 6 servings.

POTATOES IN A TRADITIONAL SCALLOP

2	tbsp. butter	2	c. milk
2	tbsp. flour	¼	c. finely chopped onion
½	tsp. salt	3	potatoes
¼	tsp. pepper		

NOTE: Milk tends to boil over in the MW so be sure to use an extra large casserole and use only (PL7) 70% power.

Peel potatoes and cut into slices, trying to make them approximately the same thickness. Put butter in a 3 or 4 quart covered casserole and MW FP 45 seconds or until melted. Whisk in milk. Add flour, spices and onion. Cover and MW PL7 for 10 minutes. Add potatoes, cover and MW PL7 for 17 - 20 minutes, stirring once halfway through the cooking time. Let stand, covered, 10 minutes.

POTATOES MASHED WITH A TWIST

2	med. size leeks, sliced	4	c. boiling water
1	med. onion, sliced	2	c. instant potatoes
2	tbsp. butter	1	c. whipping cream
4	chicken bouillon cubes		Salt & pepper to taste

In 2-quart casserole combine leeks, onion and butter. MW FP, uncovered, 4 minutes. Stir after 2 minutes cooking.

Dissolve bouillon cubes in boiling water. To leek mixture add chicken bouillon. MW FP 15 minutes, uncovered. Stir once halfway through cooking. Place mixture in blender. Return bouillon mixture to casserole dish. Add instant potatoes and cream. Stir well. MW FP 1 - 2 minutes or until hot. Season with salt and pepper. Serve hot. YIELD: 4 - 6 servings.

POTATOES, PARMEFRIED

3	med. potatoes	½	tsp. garlic powder
3	tbsp. butter	½	tsp. seasoned salt
¼	c. Parmesan cheese	½	tsp. paprika

Scrub potatoes, leaving skin on. Cut each potato into 8 wedges. Put butter in a large pie plate and MW FP 45 seconds or until melted. Dip wedges into melted butter and arrange in a doughnut pattern. Combine cheese and spices. Sprinkle evenly over potatoes. Cover with paper towel or waxed paper. MW FP 10 - 12 minutes until potatoes are just about tender. Let stand, covered, 3 minutes.

POTATOES WITH BUTTER CRUMB COATING

4 - 6 med. potatoes, peeled	½ c. Ritz-type
2 tbsp. margarine, melted	cracker crumbs

Roll peeled potatoes in margarine. Roll in crumbs to coat well. Arrange potatoes in baking dish. Cover with waxed paper. MW FP 7 - 10 minutes, or until potatoes are cooked. Let stand, covered, 5 minutes before serving.

POTATOES, STUFFED 'N' BAKED

4 baking potatoes (about 6 - 8 oz. each)	¼ tsp. salt
	¼ tsp. pepper
½ c. half and half	¼ tsp. dry mustard
¼ c. shredded Cheddar cheese (about 1 oz.)	¼ c. shredded Cheddar cheese (about 1 oz.)
2 tbsp. margarine or butter	⅛ tsp. paprika
2 tsp. dried parsley flakes	

Scrub potatoes. Pierce skins; place in circular pattern in microwave oven. MW FP 4 - 5 minutes. Turn over and rearrange. MW FP 4 - 5 minutes longer. Cut thin slice from the top of each potato. Scoop out inside with a spoon, leaving a thin shell. Add remaining ingredients except ¼ cup cheese and paprika to potatoes. Mash until no lumps remain.

Spoon ¼ of the potato mixture into each shell. Place stuffed potatoes in square baking dish, 8 x 8 inches. Sprinkle with remaining ¼ cup cheese and the paprika.

MW PL7 until cheese is melted and potatoes are heated through, 3 - 4 minutes. YIELD: 4 servings.

POTATOES - QUICK SCALLOPED

10 oz. can cream of mushroom soup	5 med. sized potatoes
	Salt & pepper to taste
½ c. sour cream (salad cream)	1 egg
	½ c. grated Cheddar cheese

Scrub potatoes. Pierce and place in a ring pattern, 1-inch apart in oven. MW FP 10 minutes until potatoes are done, but still firm. When the potatoes are done, remove from oven and immerse in cold water. While the potatoes are cooking prepare the sauce by combining the remaining ingredients in a 4-cup measure and whisking to blend. Remove the potatoes from the cold water, peel and slice thinly. Arrange half of the potatoes in a ring mold and pour half the soup mixture over them. Put the rest of the potato slices on top and add the balance of the sauce. MW PL5 for 6 - 8 minutes, uncovered. Cover and let stand 5 minutes.

POTATOES WITH MUSHROOM TOPPING

2	med. to lge. baking potatoes		Dash dill seed
½	c. water	1	tbsp. dry white wine
1	tbsp. flour	½	c. canned mushroom
½	tsp. instant chicken		pieces, drained
	bouillon		Salt
¼	tsp. salt	1	tbsp. Parmesan cheese

Scrub potatoes. Pierce skins. MW FP 4½ - 5½ minutes or until just about tender, turning potatoes over once. Set aside. Combine water, flour, bouillon, salt and dill in a 2-cup glass measure; mix well. MW FP, uncovered, 2 - 2½ minutes or until mixture boils and thickens, stirring once. Stir in wine and mushrooms. MW FP 1 - 1½ minutes or until heated through. Make a crosswise slash in each potato; press sides of potato to form an opening. Sprinkle potato with salt. Spoon mushroom mixture into potato. Sprinkle with Parmesan cheese. If necessary, reheat potatoes, 1 - 2 minutes. YIELD: 2 servings.

PUMPKIN SEEDS

This recipe may seem like there's a lot of muckin' around, but it's really not so bad, besides, that's what mothers are for, born to Muck Around! On the bright side, Hallowe'en only comes once a year and if you make it through the costume trauma you'll be in the right frame of mind for a little mindless muckin'.

Remove seeds from pumpkin. Remove muck from seeds. Wash and rinse. Add ¼ cup salt to 4 cups hot water and swish to dissolve. Add seeds and let soak overnight. Drain and rinse. Put two sheets of white paper towel on a microproof plate and arrange seeds in a ring pattern. Let stand a few hours or overnight to evaporate surface moisture. MW FP 7 - 8 minutes per cup. Never leave microwave oven unattended when drying foods in it. Let stand 5 minutes. If not dry or crisp enough return to microwave and MW FP 2 - 3 minutes. It is best to do one cup portions at a time. I love pumpkin seeds and this method of cooking is the next best to store bought I've been able to attain at home.

RICE, BROWN

1	c. parboiled long grain brown rice	1	tbsp. margarine or butter (optional)
2¾	c. hot water	1	tsp. salt

Combine all ingredients in 3-quart casserole. Cover. MW FP 5 minutes. MW PL5 until liquid is absorbed and rice is tender, 25 - 35 minutes. Fluff with fork before serving. YIELD: 4 servings.

RICE, FRIED

2 tbsp. chopped onion
1 tbsp. margarine or butter
2 tsp. instant chicken bouillon
1⅔ c. hot water
2 c. uncooked instant rice

2 tbsp. finely chopped green onion
2 eggs, beaten
1 tbsp. plus 2 tsp. soya sauce

Combine onion and margarine in 2-quart caserole. MW FP 1 - 3 minutes or until onion is tender. Set aside.

Stir bouillon into hot water until dissolved. Add bouillon mixture, rice and green onion to casserole; cover. MW FP until mixture boils, 4 - 8 minutes. Let stand, covered, until liquid is absorbed, 5 - 6 minutes.

Stir in eggs and soya sauce. MW FP, uncovered, until eggs are set, 2 - 4½ minutes, stirring several times during cooking. Fluff with fork before serving. YIELD: 4 - 6 servings.

RICE MEXICANO

1 c. rice
19 oz. can tomatoes
¼ tsp. sweet basil
  Dash garlic powder

¼ tsp. celery salt
½ tsp. oregano
2 tbsp. butter
1 c. water

In 2-quart covered casserole combine all ingredients. Mix thoroughly. MW FP 6 minutes. Stir well. MW PL4 for 15 minutes or until rice is tender. Let stand 5 minutes before serving. YIELD: 4 servings.

RICE PILAF I

¼ c. chopped onion
¼ c. chopped celery
¼ c. chopped green pepper
2 tbsp. margarine or butter
1 c. hot water

4 oz. can sliced mushrooms, drained
⅓ c. uncooked long grain rice
1 tbsp. instant chicken bouillon

Combine onion, celery, green pepper and margarine in 1-quart casserole. MW FP until vegetables are tender-crisp, 3 - 5 minutes. Stir in remaining ingredients; cover.

MW FP 5 minutes. MW PL5 for 10 - 12 minutes or until liquid is absorbed. Let stand, covered, 5 minutes. Fluff with fork before serving. YIELD: 2 - 3 servings.

RICE PILAF II

1	c. uncooked long grain rice	2	c. water
2	tbsp. butter or margarine	2	chicken bouillon cubes
¼	c. finely chopped green onion	⅓	c. sliced fresh mushrooms
¼	c. finely chopped celery	½	c. frozen peas

Combine rice and butter in a 1½ quart casserole. MW PL7 for 2 - 3 minutes, stirring once.

Add celery and green onion. MW FP 1 minute.

Add water and bouillon cubes. Stir well and cover. MW FP 5 minutes, MW PL4 for 16 - 18 minutes.

Stir in mushrooms and peas. Let stand, covered, for 10 minutes. Fluff with fork. YIELD: 4 servings.

RICE, LONG GRAIN

1	c. uncooked long grain rice	2	c. hot water
1	tbsp. margarine or butter (optional)	1	tsp. salt

Combine all ingredients in 2-quart casserole. Cover. MW FP 5 minutes. Reduce power to MW PL5 until liquid is absorbed and rice is tender, 10 - 13 minutes. Fluff with fork before serving. YIELD: 4 servings.

RICE - WILD RICE MEDLEY

1½	c. uncooked long grain & wild rice	¼	c. butter or margarine
5	c. hot water	8	oz. fresh mushrooms, sliced
½	c. chopped onion	1	tbsp. instant chicken bouillon granules
½	c. finely chopped celery		

Rinse rice in a wire strainer under cold running water. In 5-quart casserole, combine rice and hot water; cover. MW FP 30 - 35 minutes, or until rice is tender and fluffy, stirring every 10 minutes. Let rice stand, covered, 15 minutes.

In 2-quart casserole, combine onion, celery and butter; cover. MW FP 2 - 4 minutes, or until onion is tender-crisp. Stir in mushrooms and bouillon granules. MW FP 2 - 3 minutes, or until heated. Drain and rinse rice. Mix with vegetables; cover. MW FP 3 - 4 minutes, or until heated.

WILD RICE WITH MUSHROOMS AND ALMONDS

1	c. wild rice	2	tbsp. chopped green onion
¼	c. butter	2 -	10 oz. cans mushroom
½	c. blanched slivered		pieces & stems, drained
	almonds	3	c. chicken broth

Rinse rice three times under cold water. Stir rice into 3 cups boiling water. MW FP 1 minute. Soak in same water 1 hour at room temperature. Drain.

Place rice, butter, almonds, onion and mushrooms in 1½-quart glass, casserole dish. Cover. MW FP 5 minutes. Stir twice. Add chicken broth to casserole. Stir. Cover tightly. MW PL7 30 - 45 minutes or until rice is cooked. YIELD: 6 - 8 servings.

RICE WITH FRESH PARSLEY

1	lge. onion, chopped	1½	c. uncooked long grain rice
1	tbsp. olive oil or butter	¾	c. snipped fresh parsley
¾	tsp. dried basil leaves	1½	tsp. salt
¼	tsp. dried thyme leaves	¼	tsp. pepper
3	c. hot water		

Place onion, olive oil, basil and thyme in 3-quart casserole. MW FP, covered, 2½ - 4 minutes, or until onion is tender. Stir in remaining ingredients; cover.

MW FP 5 minutes. MW PL5 for 12 - 17 minutes, or until rice is tender and liquid is absorbed. Let stand 5 - 10 minutes. Fluff with fork. YIELD: 6 - 8 servings.

RUTABAGA (TURNIP) IN SOUR CREAM AND DILL

4	c. cubed rutabaga (turnip)	2	tbsp. butter
¼	tsp. salt	1	c. sour cream
	Dash pepper	½	tsp. dill seed OR
1	med. onion, sliced	1	tbsp. fresh dill

Put rutabaga in a casserole with ½ cup water. Cover. MW FP 8 - 10 minutes. Let stand 3 minutes. Drain. Sprinkle with salt and pepper. Put butter and onion in a microproof bowl. MW FP 2 minutes. Add to sour cream. Pour entire mixture over rutabaga. Sprinkle with fresh dill. YIELD: 6 servings.

RUTABAGA (TURNIP) WHIP

3   c. pared & cubed rutabaga   ¼   c. light cream
    (turnip)   ¼   c. butter or margarine
3   c. pared & cubed potatoes   Salt & pepper to taste
2   tbsp. chopped onion

Put rutabaga, potatoes, onion and ¾ cup water in a microproof casserole. MW FP 18 minutes. Let stand 3 minutes. Drain and mash rutabaga, potatoes and onion with cream and butter until light and fluffy. Season to taste with salt and pepper. YIELD: 4 - 6 servings.

SALAD DRESSED IN HOT SWEET AND SOUR DRESSING

3   strips bacon, cooked crisp   1   tbsp. white vinegar
    & crumbled   ½   c. sour cream
2   eggs   (commercially prepared)
2   tbsp. white sugar   1   tbsp. bacon drippings

Whisk eggs. Whisk in sugar, vinegar and bacon drippings. Whisk a couple of tablespoons of this mixture into the sour cream and continue to do so until all is mixed with the sour cream. Add crumbled bacon. MW FP 1 minute. Whisk. MW FP 1 minute. Pour over prepared salad.

SALAD

1   small head Romaine lettuce   1   thinly sliced sweet Spanish
10 fresh mushrooms, washed   onion
    & sliced

Wash and dry lettuce. Tear into bite sized pieces and toss into salad bowl with mushrooms and onions. Add warm salad dressing and toss well to coat vegetables.

STIR FRIES

1   tbsp. vegetable oil   2   c. fresh bean spouts,
2   small onions, wedged into   rinsed with boiling water
    eighths   ½   c. boiling water
1   c. diagonally sliced celery 1   pinch sugar
1   c. julienned green pepper   3   tbsp. light soya sauce
2   c. shredded Chinese   1   bouillon cube
    cabbage   2   tbsp. tapioca starch

Put oil in a 3-quart covered casserole and MW FP 1 minute. Add prepared vegetables, cover and MW FP 3 minutes. Stir. MW FP 2 minutes. Prepare sauce by dissolving tapioca starch in ¼ cup cold water. Put bouillon cube in boiling water along with sugar and soya sauce. Stir tapioca mixture into bouillon mixture. Pour over vegetables. Cover and MW FP 3 minutes. Stir. MW FP 3 minutes. Let stand 5 minutes.

STUFFED MUSHROOM CAPS

8	oz. fresh mushrooms	1	tsp. Worcestershire sauce
2	tbsp. butter	1	tsp. parsley flakes
¼	c. finely chopped celery	¼	tsp. salt
¼	c. finely chopped onion	⅛	tsp. oregano
¼	c. dry bread crumbs		

Wash mushrooms. Remove and chop stems. Combine stems, butter and vegetables in bowl. MW FP 1½ - 2½ minutes, or until vegetables are tender-crisp, stirring once. Stir in remaining ingredients. Mound into mushroom caps. Arrange caps on paper towel-lined plate. MW FP 1½ - 3 minutes, or until thoroughly heated, rotating plate once or twice. Serve warm.

SUNSHINE BRUSSELS SPROUTS

2 -	10 oz. pkgs. frozen Brussels sprouts	¼	c. half and half
2	tbsp. water	2	egg yolks, slightly beaten
¼	c. chopped onion	1	tbsp. fresh lemon juice
1	tbsp. margarine or butter	⅛	tsp. salt
			Dash pepper

Place Brussels sprouts and water in 2-quart casserole; cover. MW FP until tender, 8 - 10 minutes, stirring after half the cooking time. Drain and set aside.

Place onion and margarine in 2-cup measure. MW FP until onion is tender, 1 - 2 minutes. Blend in remaining ingredients.

MW PL7 until thickened, 30 seconds to 2 minutes, stirring every 30 seconds. Pour over Brussels sprouts. MW FP until heated through, 1 minute. YIELD: 4 - 6 servings.

TOMATO PARMESAN

2	tomatoes, cut in half	Parmesan cheese
	Basil	Croutons, crushed

Cut edge of tomato halves with sharp knife at ¼ inch intervals to make zig-zag effect. Sprinkle with basil, Parmesan cheese and crushed croutons. Cover with transparent wrap. MW FP 30 seconds. YIELD: 4 tomato halves.

SUPER CYN'S SOUPER ZUCCHINI

Super Cyn, a kitchen whiz. Her favorite trick is to whiz out of the kitchen as quickly as is humanly possible.

With a job, two tots and a husband who is pickier than Morris the Cat, Cynthia has to find recipes that are quick and appealing. This one is a sure winner.

2 or 3 evenly sliced zucchini	½ can condensed tomato soup
1 med. onion, diced	
3 ribs celery sliced on 45° angle	1 lb. grated Mozzarella cheese
1 carrot, grated	¼ tsp. salt
1 clove fresh garlic OR	⅛ tsp. pepper
¼ tsp. garlic powder	

Toss vegetables into 9 x 13 inch baking dish. Add minced fresh garlic or garlic powder to UNDILUTED tomato soup along with salt and pepper.Pour over vegetables. Sprinkle cheese over top.

MW FP 10 minutes. If you wish to brown the cheese, pop the casserole under the broiler for a few minutes.

THREE BEAN BAKE

4 slices bacon	1 med. onion, sliced
1 tbsp. shortening or bacon fat	14 oz. can cut green beans, drained
⅓ c. sugar	14 oz. can cut wax beans, drained
1 tbsp. cornstarch	
1 tsp. salt	14 oz. can red kidney beans, drained
⅛ tsp. pepper	
½ c. vinegar	

Place bacon slices on rack or a plate in microwave oven. Cover with waxed paper. Cook 3 - 4 minutes or until crisp.

Drain bacon on a paper towel. Add shortening or bacon fat to 2-quart casserole.

Mix sugar, cornstarch, salt and pepper with fat. Stir in vinegar. Add remaining ingredients. Mix well.

MW FP 10 minutes or until sauce has thickened. Stir several times during cooking period. Crumble bacon over top. YIELD: 4 - 6 servings.

VEGETABLE MEDLEY WITH BECHAMEL SAUCE

2	carrots, cut in thin strips	2	c. cauliflowerets
2	c. broccoli flowerets	1	c. Hubbard, butternut
1	small zucchini, thinly sliced		or acorn squash, cut into wedges

Arrange cauliflower and broccoli alternately, stem ends toward edge of dish. Arrange carrot sticks to form a circle for next ring. Overlap squash and zucchini in centre of dish. Sprinkle with 3 tablespoon water, cover tightly with plastic wrap, venting one edge. MW FP 6 - 8 minutes or until tender crisp. Let stand, covered, while preparing sauce. YIELD: 4 servings.

BECHAMEL SAUCE

2	tbsp. butter or margarine	2	tsp. grated onion or instant
2	tbsp. flour		
½	c. light cream	¼	tsp. salt
½	c. chicken broth (can use bouillon dissolved)	⅛	tsp. nutmeg

Put butter in 4-cup measure. MW FP 30 seconds or until melted. Whisk in flour, blending until smooth. Add onion and seasonings. Whisk in chicken broth and cream. MW FP, stirring 2 or 3 times, for 2½ to 3 minutes, until thickened.

VEGETABLE SKILLET

2	tbsp. butter	½	tsp. salt
½	c. chopped onion	¼	tsp. curry powder
2	med. zucchini	¼	tsp. powdered ginger
3	med. tomatoes, wedged		Dash pepper
6	mushrooms, sliced		

Put butter in a 1½-quart casserole and MW FP until melted. Add onion and zucchini and cover. MW FP 3 minutes, stirring after every minute. Stir in tomatoes, mushrooms and seasonings. Cover, MW FP 3 minutes, stirring halfway through cooking time. Let stand, covered, 5 minutes.

Tea Refreshments for 300 people:

12 large sandwich loaves, sliced lengthwise (6 white & 6 brown)

Fillings For Fancy Sandwiches
Ribbon & Rolled:

4 dozen eggs — hard boil, make filling with salad dressing and seasoning.

4 tins Klik or 1 lb. of ham or bologna — Mix with salad dressing and dills, chopped or sweet relish. This can be used for rolled sandwiches or ribbon type with egg, using alternate layers of white and brown bread.

1½ lbs. white cream cheese — Mix with salad dressing. Spread on bread. Sprinkle with chopped maraschino cherries. Make in rolls. Takes 1 - 12 oz. jar red cherries and 1 - 6 oz green.

1½ lbs. Velveeta — Mix with salad dressing. Make in rolls with olives (takes about 4 per slice) or dill slices.

3 tins shrimp — Mix with salad dressing. Roll.

2 large tins salmon — Mix with chopped celery, salad dressing and seasoning. Roll centered with dill.

These should be tightly rolled in wax paper and refrigerated till cut. These amounts will make 800 sandwiches allowing 2-3 per person.

Dainties for 300 people:

3 per person usually allowed. 25 persons supplying 3 dozen each should be sufficient if a group project.

Also required: 2 lbs. tea - 3 lbs. sugar cubes - 3 qts. creamilk - ½ gallon sweet pickles - ½ gallon dills.

SUPPER QUANTITY COOKING

BAKED BEANS FOR 100:

8 qts. dry beans	4 lbs. salt pork
20 qts. salad	20 doz. rolls
4 lbs. butter	20 pies
4 qts. cream	2 lbs. coffee

HASH SUPPER FOR 100:

40 lbs. corned beef	5 qts. salad dressing
32 qts. potatoes	4 lbs. butter
20 doz. rolls	2 lbs. coffee
20 qts. chopped cabbage	4 qts. cream

CABBAGE SALAD FOR 175:

20 lbs. cabbage	4 large cans crushed
1½ qts. salad dressing	pineapple
	2 bunches carrots

CHICKEN SHORTCAKE FOR 135:

60 lbs. chicken	3 large pkg. Bisquick
30 pkgs. frozen peas	17 pkgs. Flakon corn mix
12 cans cranberry sauce	2 bunches celery

HAM SUPPER FOR 225:

48 lbs. canned ham	45 qts. strawberries
24 potato salads	6 pkgs. Bisquick (mixed
(solicited)	re directions for
48 pkgs. peas (1 lb.)	shortcake)
5 lbs. coffee	6 qts. heavy cream
9 qts. cream	

BRAISED BEEF FOR 200:

65 lbs. stew beef	Harvard beets
60 lbs. potatoes	40 lbs. turnips
36 pies	2 lbs. cheese

TURKEY DINNER FOR 250:

7 turkeys	75 lbs. potatoes
75 lbs. butternut squash	10 bunches celery
20 large cranberry rings	44 pies

Pot Pourri o' Cook Books

One can never be too wealthy. Expand on the wealth of your cooking knowledge without going broke in the process . . .

Gateway is North America's most diversified FUND RAISING PUBLISHER. Because of the tremendous volume of cook books that we publish each year, we accumulate a large stock of overruns. As a result, we have put these books into assortment packs and are offering them for sale at 60% off the selling price. The books will be of the same, fine quality as this one, with full color section dividers and spiral binding and can originate from any corner of North America. Although we cannot guarantee precisely which books you will receive, we do guarantee they will be interesting and that no duplicates will be in any individual assortment.

ORDER FORM

Enclosed please find my check _____ for _____ books

1 Book for $ 3.95 _____   10 Books for $24.95 _____

3 Books for $ 9.95 _____   15 Books for $34.95 _____

5 Books for $14.95 _____   20 Books for $39.95 _____

Please send to M. _____

Address _____
                                             Town

_____
State/Prov.   Zip Code/Postal Code

In Canada send to:
Gateway Publishing Co. Ltd.
811 Pandora Avenue, West, Box 220
Transcona P.O., Winnipeg, Manitoba
Canada R2C 2Z9

In United States send to:
Gateway Publishing Co., Inc.
276 Cavalier Street, P.O. Box 698
Pembina, North Dakota
U.S.A. 58271-0698

PLEASE CUT OUT AND MAIL CARD FOR INFORMATION

Canadian residents please use this one

For information on how easily you or your organization can raise money with a personalized cook book or one of our many other fund raising publications, please fill out this card and return it to us for your kit on the Gateway method to fund raising.

CHECK ONE ONLY:

☐ Personalized Cook Book
☐ Wild Game Cook Book I
☐ Wild Game Cook Book II
☐ Community or Family History Book
☐ Cut a Little . . . Save a Lot

☐ Fighting Back
☐ Personal Hockey Memories
☐ Personal Baseball Memories
☐ Soccer Memories
☐ Figure Skating Memories
☐ Gateway to Microwaving

The information should go to: M _____

Address _____
Street or Box Number

of _____
Town   Province   Postal Code

Organization is _____

of _____
Town   Province   Postal Code

My Name is _____ of _____
Town   Province

Phone _____ Date _____

CUT RIGHT ON DOTTED LINES

U.S. residents please use this one

For information on how easily you or your organization can raise money with a personalized cook book or one of our many other fund raising publications, please fill out this card and return it to us for your kit on the Gateway method to fund raising.

CHECK ONE ONLY:

☐ Personalized Cook Book
☐ Wild Game Cook Book I
☐ Wild Game Cook Book II
☐ Community or Family History Book
☐ Cut a Little . . . Save a Lot

☐ Fighting Back
☐ Personal Hockey Memories
☐ Personal Baseball Memories
☐ Soccer Memories
☐ Figure Skating Memories
☐ Gateway to Microwaving

The information should go to: M _____

Address _____
Street or Box Number

of _____
Town   State   Zip Code

Organization is _____

of _____
Town   State   Zip Code

My Name is _____ of _____
Town   State

Phone _____ Date _____

GATEWAY PUBLISHING CO. LTD.

811 Pandora Avenue West,
Box 220 Transcona, P.O.
Winnipeg, Manitoba, Canada
R2C 9Z9

GATEWAY PUBLISHING CO., INC.

276 Cavalier Street, P.O. Box 698
Pembina, North Dakota
U.S. 58271-0698

CRETE

(402) 826-5167

LINCOLN

(402) 474-7816

BOX 322, CRETE, NE 68333

COOK UP A GOOD BUY FROM JACK KEEFS GM OUTLET

PONTIAC, OLDS, BUICK & CHEVROLET

826-5167

CRETE, NEBRASKA

Crete
Municipal Hospital

PHONE: (402) 826-2154

1540 GROVE STREET, P.O. BOX 220, CRETE, NE 68333